We're All Mad Here

marie kuipers

We're All Mad Here

an (in)elegant memoir

First Edition 2024

Paperback ISBN: 978-1-990700-62-0
eBook ISBN: 978-1-990700-61-3

Library of Congress Control Number: 2024916069

Interior design by Kevin Coleman
Cover design by Tabitha Rose

Printed in the U.S.A.
1 2 3 4 5 6 7 8 9 10

Life to Paper Publishing Inc.
Toronto | Miami

https://lifetopaper.com/

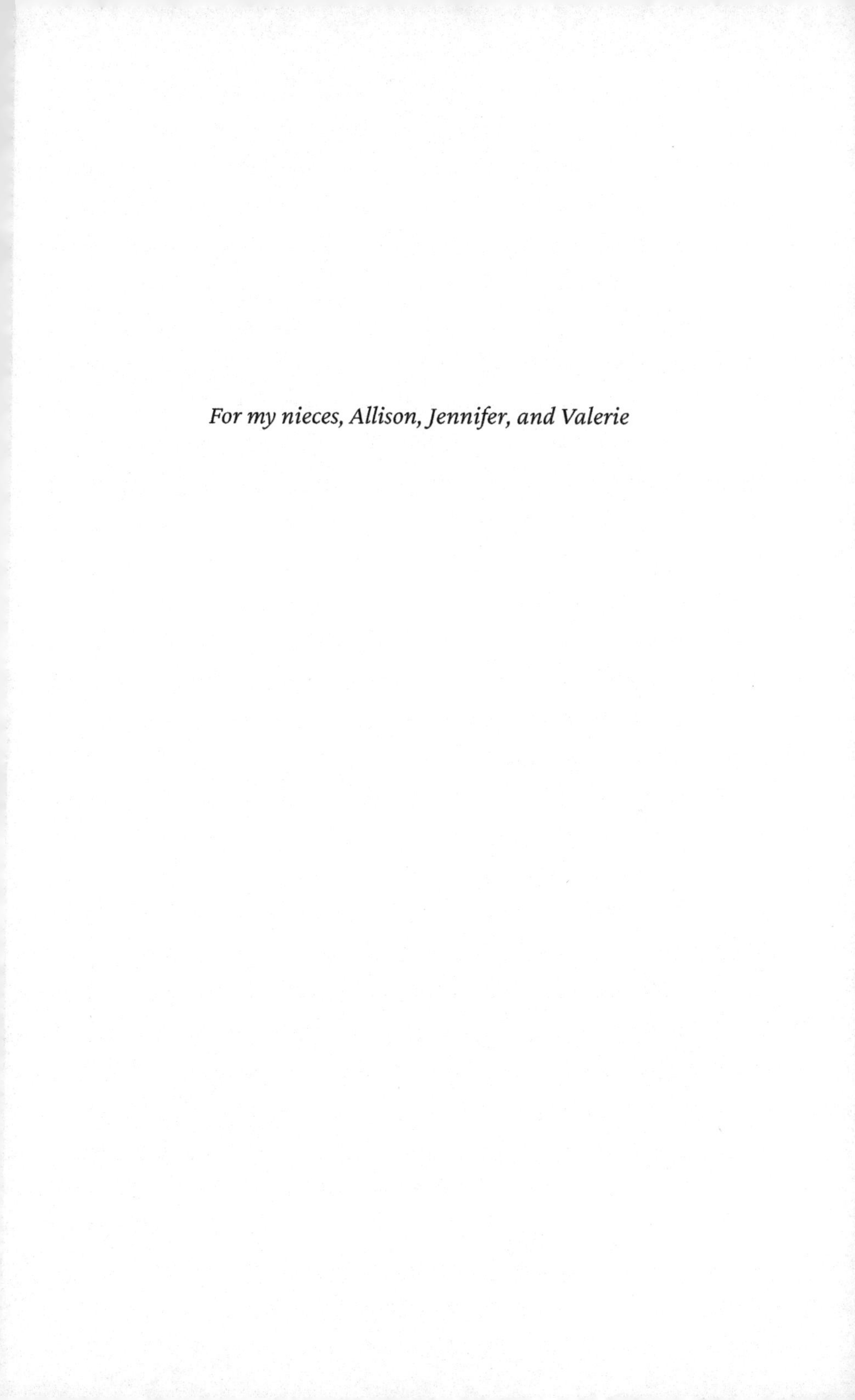

For my nieces, Allison, Jennifer, and Valerie

contents

1 / a quick primer on my grumpy ass

Dear Reader: Welcome to the shit show. I'm delighted you're here. If we are to get to know each other (and I hope we are), it's only fair that I should warn you about a few things. First of all, I am a hot, steaming mess of a human being. You need to know this before you proceed. I'm ornery, irritable, cynical, and sarcastic. In my defense, I'm a product of some pretty bonkers familial trauma, which has colored my perception of nearly everything I encounter (said color is, obviously, a deep, shit-stain brown) and has made it difficult to ascertain whether I'm a massive dickhead damaged beyond repair or just adorably jerky, like a Welsh corgi. That is for you to decide. I find most people objectionable, because, let's face it, most people suck. (You are clearly not "most people." You have exquisite taste in books, and those jeans make your ass look ahmazing.)

Most people are cruel, careless, selfish, and generally disappointing. I like to think that I'm not any of those things, but chances are I'll offend and/or disappoint you at some point (just ask my mother). Sorry about that. Lucky for you, I am also hilarious.

I'm kind to children (unless they fuck with me, obviously)

and old people. My nieces and my animals are the things I live for, and I'm at my best when they need me. I'm also a really good—and, dare I say, delightful?—friend, loyal and true. I have to be, to make up for all the assholery.

Before I expound on said assholery, I'm going to give some mad snaps to some of the things that get me through the worst of times with most of my soul intact, and that have the power, at least for me, to turn the most tedious of tasks into awesome-adjacent antics. That's as high as my personal happiness needle goes, and these are a few of things that get me there.

Halloween. I stopped taking down my Halloween decorations years ago, because my heart is dark and twisty all year round, and why shouldn't my home reflect my terrifying essence? My house is unsubtly festooned with witch hats, skulls, graveyard art, and pumpkin-shaped crockery at all times. Also, obviously, candy. King-sized. Because who the fuck thought they could gaslight children into believing that the tiniest, most pathetic little nuggets of life-affirming chocolate are "fun-sized"? Absolute horse shit.

British crime shows. These streaming-service gems are not only gritty, atmospheric, and brilliantly crafted, but they also serve to remind me that no matter how dark and doomy I fancy myself, the British are here to remind me that I am a goddamn ray of sunshine compared to their ghastly, murder-loving asses.

Farts. If I need to explain to you why farts are hilarious, this may not be the book for you. It's the wholesomest, cheapest, playing-field-levelingest delight that exists in humankind. Farts are always funny. Always. (Also? I make up words. And I'm not sorry.)

Proper fucking carbs. There is literally nothing finer on earth than some chewy-noodle or crusty-bread action, and no one will ever convince me otherwise. I hold this truth as my personal North Star, so please don't @ me with your gelatinous mung-bean pasta atrocities. It will not work and I will write you off as an unhinged lunatic. If you are someone who cannot medically consume gluten, my heart truly breaks for you. I hope you have something in your life that brings you the kind of joy I'm talking about. I doubt it, though.

Salt and vinegar kettle chips. Yes, this technically falls into the above category, but a good salt 'n vinnie chip offers a sour, salty transcendence that really nothing else can touch. And the shit that's left over on your fingers after you kill a bag of S 'n Vs is something I would gladly slather over my entire body and lick for days on end if I could. Not that I've tried it. *Why, what did you hear?*

If you can roll with me on these few things, I guarantee you'll get the best version of me that's currently available. This is some friends-for-life shit, and I don't say that lightly. BFFFs.

Admittedly, however, I can also be a bit of a dickhole. But I promise you with my whole heart that I'm only a dickhole when dickhole-being is called for, as it often is. Otherwise, I am truly content to live and let live.

Express your truest self! Fuck anyone who doesn't like it.

Love and marry exactly whom you want to love and marry—everyone deserves that. Everyone.

Worship whatever and wherever you choose. (Extra credit if there's a Pan-flute-playing goat god involved, or some secret woodland negotiations between you and your local forest witches' union. I want details.) Enjoy your shit and respect my right to enjoy my own shit.

But mess with my people? Wrong my pets? Prepare to be served with the full wrath and authority of my feral, majestic ass. Shock and awe, motherfuckers. Shock and awe. Mostly shock. That they let the crazy lady out again.

If you'd like to avoid this ever-so-slightly less charming

version of me, there are a few things you may want to steer clear of. So let's get to it, shall we? I don't have all day.

Bad grammar. This is a big one, and the surest, most reliable way to torment me. I don't tolerate misspellings, and will boycott without hesitation any business, product, or person who abuses apostrophes (please note: There is no apostrophe in "apostrophes") or who cannot get a handle on basic homophones (like there, their, they're).

Mind you, I am not opposed to lazy texting or conversationally appropriate missteps. I mean, you obviously sound like a way bigger dickhead saying things like "There are things up with which I simply will not put" than you would if you just rolled with that floating preposition. The trick is to know the difference.

I am a copy editor by trade, so technically your grammatical war crimes put food in my belly. So while professionally I welcome them with open compounds and closed brackets, in real life I'm gonna need you to get your shit together. Let's move on. This is exhausting.

Judgy hipsters. Yes, dude. I forgot my reusable hemp sack. But I'm pretty sure those edgy nonprescription spectacles of yours will be sitting in the landfill longer than this plastic grocery bag for which I just had to prostrate myself. So bite me, bro.

Also? I'm judging you, too. For your cultivated superiority, for the way you scorn and condescend to anyone less accomplished than you, anyone who isn't urban foraging or eating bespoke wild-crafted, plant-based buttholes. Anyone who doesn't pretentiously snap their fingers at your original spoken-word poetry reading at a shitty bar in rural Vermont. I am judging you right back. It's happening silently in my brain, but it's brutal. So maybe we're even.

Chewing. No one wants to hear it—least of all me. The

sound that you and your wet, masticating mouth-hole make when you eat is something that should stay between you and your gods. The rest of us would simply like to exist in a world where the moist, rhythmic commingling of your saliva and your snack selection stays silent. That's right. *Moist.* Loud chewing makes you the sensory equivalent of the worst word in the world.

The second-worst word in the English language happens to be "mouthfeel." This is not a coincidence. Do not ever, for any reason, tell me what is going on in your mouth. What's that? It's watering? It's dry? Keep that shit to yourself. Jesus.

Things that sound delicious, but aren't. For example, sweetbreads. Black pudding. Urinal cakes. Head cheese. Spoiler alert: That's not pudding. Or cake. Or cheese.

I can trace several of my many dozen trust issues back to these deceptive culinary run-ins, including every single time I've bitten into a cookie only to find that *those aren't chocolate chips, motherfucker.* Just don't mess with my food. Ever. It's all I've got to live for.

Confederate flags. It's time to let go, folks. It's not a "Southern thing." It's a racist thing. It has no place in this country, on your truck, or as a tiny racist bikini stretched to within an inch of its life across your giant, pendulous teats. I beg you. Find some other way to show your regional pride.

Nouns used as verbs. Parent. Action. Journal. Plate. Medal. All nouns. There are lots of lovely verbs out there that express these things without violating the laws of all that is good and holy. The reverse is also appalling: "Ask" is a verb. *A verb, I tell you!* Don't fuck with me on this. I will crush you.

A quick rundown of daily irritants that I struggle to share a planet with: self-righteous vegans, tailgaters (the driving kind, not the partying kind), the word "manscaping," racists, homophobes, stinging nettles, celebrity perfumes, Marjorie Taylor

Greene, most kinds of squash, adorable kid singers, people who say, "bru-SHET-uh" (it's bru-SKET-uh), licky envelopes, dudebros, and mean girls.

Finally, there's one last thing that you should definitely know for your own health and safety: I become dangerously unhinged by the word "brownout." As should you.

Obviously, friends, this is only a partial list and barely puts a dent in the mountain of things that annoy me. But I feel in my twisted, infernal heart that it's important for you to know what you're getting into so you can decide whether you want to keep reading. I hope you will. But I totally get it if you don't. As my mother always made sure to remind me, *I'm not for everyone.*

If you are a puppies-and-rainbows purist, I'd suggest getting an immediate refund. If you like your puppies and rainbows with a side of poop talk, sexting, the occasional stalker, and an all-you-can-eat profanity buffet, you sound like my kind of asshole. And if you're fascinated by the ways that a whole mess of trauma informs one's personal development (aka "How Crazy Is Made"), I do hope you'll read on. It's a motherfucking trainwreck. If that's your thing, stick around. You're gonna love it.

And I think you and I will get along just fine.

2 / made in jersey, enjoyed everywhere

AHHH, THE MOTHERLAND. The Garden State. The Dirty Jerz (Ol' Derty, if you're nasty). The sweet, filthy land of ~~milk and honey~~ swamp and pork roll. I'm sure I don't need to remind you of the many culinary, musical, and theatrical delights offered up by my homeland, but I will, because bragging is fun: Bruce. Meryl. Whitney. Jack. Shaquille. Frank. Taylor (ham, that is). Our human legends don't even need last names.

We Jersey folk are special, and we know it (and no—I'm not making air quotes around the word "special"). I mean, how many other states have multiple movies and television shows devoted solely to the antics of their hair salons, beaches, bakeries, housewives, and Cosa Nostra underworld?

None, I tell you.

Not one.

Aside: I recently learned that in Japan, the Jersey Shore *TV series is called* Macaroni Rascals, *and I can't currently think of anything that has left me so sublimely shook. Chef's kiss perfection.*

No other state in the Union has more attitude, more pride, more corruption, or more baked-in aggression than NJ. We love our fuckin' sports, our fuckin' legends, our fuckin' beaches, and our fuckin' food. We know what matters and where you can stick it. And on that particular subject, can we get some goddamn commotion for the four Jersey goons who made away with a tractor-trailer load of pasta? Not all heroes wear capes. Some wear *moppine*. So's not to get sauce on the undashirt.

But I digress—we are Jerseyans. We've seen things. We've done things. We've smelled things.

When life or love (or the law) drives us across state lines in any sort of permanent capacity, we are, many of us, lost. Misunderstood. Judged for our fierce honesty and IDGAF confidence, which appears to frighten meeker species encountered in the wild. Deal with it, mofos. You know that if you were ever in need of a ferocious honor-defender or battle-ready blood-feud architect, you'd call us first. And we'd show up. It might be after a quick pit stop at the Bendix for some disco fries, but we'd fucking be there.

I've lived in a lot of other places as well, some more hospitable than others. I've lived where, during huntin' season, one's crucial accessory is not aggressively embossed eyebrows or high-end hooker boots, but a safety-orange Elmer Fudd hat. So's not to get shot. (And while we're on the subject of Michigan, I just need to say that despite being strongly in favor of equal-opportunity everything, I still have this wee needling feeling that giving blind people hunting licenses is in no one's best interest. Except maybe the deer's.) This is also the place where I discovered human shit in my front yard. Twice.

And you think Jersey is gross.

I've lived in places where I've gone a week without seeing another human, and have had to wonder if I really wanted to anyway, when no one's company could possibly be as goddamned delightful as my own or my Jersey brethren's. I've been imprisoned for days by end-times weather and enticed by tiny ghost-twins to come and play with them forever. And ever. And ever.

I've lived where octogenarians are driven to assault one another over a bag of ice during hurricane season—where elbow bones sweat and twenty-four-hour curfews are enforced until the "snake situation" is under control. And not a decent slice in sight.

I've had to wait in line at gas station restrooms behind bands of prairie-clad sister wives while their collective husband (singular) gassed up the tricked-out minivan and stocked up on canned goods for the compound.

I've spent actual time devising plans to scare away indefatigable missionaries come to save my sorry soul—plans that usually involve alcohol, obscenities, and ritual virgin sacrifice ... Well, shit, maybe they're right.

I've lived in positively lovely places, too. In the embrace of majestic mountains with fluffy snowfalls and fragrant evergreens; by the sea with its astounding vastness and salty quintessence; in glittering cities alive with lust and hunger, music and magic. But none of them is home. And none of them could keep me for long.

The fact is, I am quite ill-prepared to handle my fiery Jersey intensity outside state lines. Bird flipping, high-volume profanity, and making "offers they can't refuse" don't seem to be effective life strategies in the lesser states. I am a veritable fish out of water almost everywhere I go (or, as I like to think of it, an anchovy out of its extra-virgin) and have little grasp on who I am and how to be. Like, how many times do I have to say, "I'M NOT YELLING—I'M FROM NEW JERSEY" before people understand that this is just how I talk?

While I won't pretend to hail from any part of my soul state's more unsavory echelons—my hometown is distressingly posh and I have no accent to speak of, because life is a cruel mistress—I can claim some peripheral street cred, thanks to my sweet old Italian nanny, who came to help take care of me when I was two and just never left. Missy. She was the fucking *bombina*. She drank straight whiskey, smoked a pack of Parliaments a day, and taught me how to cook, play cards, and curse in Italian. She was part of my family and I was part of hers.

Missy had a son, Tony, who worked as a hired heavy for some lower-tier wannabe boss in order to pay off his (Tony's) gambling debts. Most Friday afternoons (payday for Missy), he'd show up at the house to pick up an envelope full of cash from her pay. I would hand him the envelope if she wasn't around, and he always signed off with "C'mere, kid. I love ya. Don't tell nobody I was here," along with a smack upside the head. Absolute heaven.

Missy died when I was twenty-two. I wore black for a month, which seemed fitting in a Victorian era, Italian widow kind of way. I'm not certain what became of Tony. Theirs was the NJ that taught me to love NJ. And it's the home I miss when I'm elsewhere. Family. Loyalty. Sunday gravy. Some light racketeering.

I mean, at that home? There's no call to "forgive those who trespass against us." One simply goes outside with one's baseball bat and says, loudly and with gestures, "Why don't you come up here and say that to my face, old man!"

At home, one's holiday spirit is not nearly whole without gridlock, angry shoppers, naked threats, and perilous parking-lot aggression. It warms my icy heart just thinking about it.

I can say with some authority that no one in New Jersey has ever accidentally found herself in line at a craft store on cue-pon day, silently begging God to kill her. In NJ, it's never more than a five-minute drive to the perfect slice or some decent deli. And when you need something taken care of—

whether it be a simple paint job or something more, um, permanent—everyone's Got a Guy. And everyone understands that when your friend tells you they've Got a Guy, you don't ask questions.

Jersey grudges are nurtured loudly and lovingly, like family members, and are almost always temporary. (Exception: Bad Blood. Bad Blood is *forever.*) In NJ, Mall = Mecca. Fury = Life force.

No matter where I go that is not home, I am a stranger in a strange land—where incontinent drivers (which obviously enrage me) do not throw Slurpees out the window or make the finger-across-the-throat gesture when you give them a show of your finely honed road rage—they simply move out of the way or, God forbid, give a small, sincere, sorry-wave.

Where people bring casseroles and open doors and step aside and give up seats for others. I mean, what am I supposed to do with this bullshit? Blend?

Nowadays I dwell in the Chicago area, which is significantly more hospitable, relatively speaking, to the likes of me than most other places I've landed—places where befuddled locals whip themselves into a tsk-tsk tizzy at my Jersey grace and glory. Or run away. I'm not such an objectionable anomaly here in the Windy. I'm not sure whether it's because Chicago inspires a similarly fierce loyalty to its signature foods, gangsters, and corrupt politicians as NJ or if it's just that Chicagoans don't give a fuck about anything. They mind their damn business. Either way, it's an OK substitute for now. Until I can make my way home again.

Till that glorious day, I will keep the acrid fumes burning in my swampland soul and know that upon my triumphant return, the motherland will welcome me home with a loving smack, some soothing profanity, and a behemoth tube of

Taylor ham. And I will be able to breathe again—I mean, not literally (because pollution), but spiritually.

Assimilation is exhausting. And futile. I have legitimately tried. But still, myriad times in myriad places, I have found myself in the company of Those Less Coarse after a routine display of my regional inappropriateness as they titter nervously and resort to their banal choruses of "You can take the girl out of Jersey, but you can't take the Jersey out of the girl ..."

And to them I say, always, "Why the fuck would you want to?"

fist pump

3 / life, with a twist of lyme

Recently, a friend posted a link on Facebook to a short documentary on Lyme disease—I don't always click on these things because I know myself—I am weirdly reactive and hyper-emotional on this subject, even though it's been well over a decade since I was cured. I lost years of my life to this illness, as well as countless friends, my dignity, confidence, one husband, one almost-husband, and a burgeoning business. It was the first thing—but not the last—that would rob me of the children I wanted so badly.

I could write here for hours—nay, days, years—about my life with Lyme disease. It was awful and I really don't fucking want to talk about it. But it's important that I do.

Lyme hits everyone differently. Mine hit like a ton of bricks, except with the bricks dipped in acid and studded with satanic fire-nails. Over the course of a few days, I went from a fully functioning human being who was a week away from her wedding to a hospitalized, brain-damaged invalid. Short-term memory, gone. Use of my right arm, poof. Extensive (and exquisite, I might add) vocabulary, wiped right the fuck out. I simply peered out of my skull with eyes that could not tell my brain what was happening.

I was bedridden for months, with frequent trips back to the hospital for fluids, tests, more tests. The doctors inserted a PICC line through a vein from my elbow all the way to my heart, so I could administer my own daily intravenous medicines. The wire stuck out of me for about six months, and there was no way to even accessorize it, for fuckssake.

When I became well enough to do an occasional errand or see a friend, I would often end up having to nap in my car for fear I would not make it the five minutes home without falling asleep. Often, I would get lost in the town I'd lived in for my entire life, on streets I knew like I knew my own name. I would call my mother and tell her the names on the street signs I could see, and she would have to come find me so I could follow her back to my home. Many times, I got in my car to go ... somewhere, but I would forget where I was supposed to go. So I would go home. When I could find it.

Lyme fucked with me in ways both subtle and catastrophic. Thankfully, the catastrophics have mostly resolved over time and after years of treatment. Small things remain, like migraines (not small by any means, but smaller), sound-sensitivity, visual scrambling, and word-searching. The Lyme spirochetes decided to hang out in my gallbladder for a while, so that had to go (10/10 would recommend keeping your gallbladder if at all possible). My short-term memory is still shit, and if I really need to remember something I have to write it down or otherwise "mark" the moment.

I was forever changed by a tiny fucking bug and I'm pretty pissed about it, TBH.

So I don't usually click. This time, though, I did click and had the predicted response. Tears, weird snarfling sobs, and a strong desire to shake my fist at the sky and scream. (I didn't do that last part, OK? I swear.) It also got me so wound up that I spent the entire night in a ragey fit—for it seems that in the twenty-four years since I first became ill, nothing has changed. Not one goddamned thing. The medical community still treats Lyme like a nuisance ailment, and nothing more. Nothing to get worked up about. And now I really do want to scream. But I won't, because I am a fucking lady, thank you very much.

Instead, I will tell you my story and you can decide whether or not you want to worry about Lyme.

On September 30, 2000, what was to be my wedding day, I awoke in the emergency room of the Valley Hospital paralyzed on my right side from forehead to fingertip, with unspeakable pain in my back, neck, jaw, and head, and a life-threatening fever of nearly 105 degrees.

On the way to my rehearsal dinner the night before, I told my best friend, who was driving, that I was definitely dying, and that I just hoped it could wait until after the wedding. Nobody wanted to party with a dead bride. She flipped a bitch and bee-lined my delirious ass straight to the ER.

Once they had gotten my fever down and given me some magical fairy potion for the pain, the tests began. Blood, blood, and more blood; CAT scans, MRIs, EKGs, neurological assessments, and the *pièce de résistance*, the *spinal tap.* (My favorite movie of all time. Not my favorite medical procedure.) Have you ever had a giant bucatini-sized needle plunged into your spinal cord to retrieve a soda can full of your vertebra juice? Don't. It sucks donkey dong.

I don't remember much about those early days, but I remember the fuck outta that. I also remember the patronizing clucks of my doctors, friends, and family who deep down believed I was merely experiencing some acute pre-wedding jitters.

This was not entirely unexpected in light of the fact that in the four days preceding my trip to the ER, I had visited two MDs, two chiropractors, and one acupuncturist in search of some relief from my ever-increasing pain—only to be told repeatedly that I was suffering from wedding-related stress. One such doctor (who had not made note of the fact that my fiancé had to half carry me from the car to his office because I could not walk on my own) even dared to suggest that I "Relax and go shopping."

Would you like some flagrant misogyny to accompany your death throes, m'lady? Why yes, thank you, good sir.

Not one, including my own beloved family practitioner, bothered to take my temperature, vital signs, or blood samples. It was the masseuse I visited the day of the rehearsal, hoping to relieve some of the pain, who told me I had a temperature: "You have bad fever. Body burn like fire."

She was the only one who noticed. And she was right.

I cannot explain the others' negligence. But years later, as doctors and journalists alike continue to perpetuate the "Lyme is a myth" bullshit, I at least understand it. They don't exactly deny it exists, they just don't think it's that big a deal. Easily treatable, they say. Nothing to worry about, they say. Lyme anxiety is of much more concern than the Lyme itself, they say. "Inflated public fear" serves no one, they say.

Eat a bag of dicks, assholes. That's what I say. For it was indeed Lyme disease that uninvited me from my own wedding and very nearly took my life.

If you ask me, people aren't afraid enough. I can't count the number of well-meaning but uneducated and/or misinformed inquiries I have fielded regarding my illness: "So, uh, Lyme's disease, bruh—how did you get that? From a mosquito?" and "So, what, are you, like, tired a lot?"

My favorite, however, came from an otherwise well-educated New Jersey man: "Whoa, dude. Can you get that from limes?" Hardly inflated public fear.

I and many other Lyme patients suffer from drastic

memory loss, cognitive dysfunction, trouble speaking and thinking, constant confusion, tremor, sudden-onset dyslexia, loss of balance, paralysis, chronic arthritis, vertigo, heart damage, Bell's palsy, and countless other symptoms ranging from inconvenient to unbearable.

Add to that the abandonment of one's family and friends, who regard our memory problems as "irresponsible," our need for help and support as "selfish," and our "imaginary" fatigue as frankly tiresome, and you've got yourself a big fat shit sandwich.

Indeed, Lyme can look like lots of other things. And that's how the medical community justifies their derision and dismissal of patients like me. *Hypochondriacs. Depressives. Antibiotic junkies.*

While doctors can obviously suck it hard, there's still nothing more demoralizing than a trusted friend who dismisses your agonizing forgetfulness with inane shit like "Well, I must have it then, too, 'cause I'm like that all the time LOL!"

And I had lots of those friends. The friends who told me I'd feel better if I got out of bed and went for a run; that I should definitely drink more water; that I should buy $600 of essential oils from them and also try their shrink. *He's the best in town. He'll figure out what's wrong with you.*

Now, all these years later, I still get triggered as fuck by Lyme ignorance. Along with many other insidious offenders, Lyme is an invisible disease. No one can tell by looking at you that your body and your mind and your life are absolutely FUCKED. *You don't look sick,* they'd say. Which was likely meant to reassure me that I was keeping my outer shit tight even if everything beneath my skin was in major malfunction. But it was not reassuring. It was dismissive. It was cruel.

When I was at my sickest and all anyone could say was that I still "looked amazing," I often considered using crutches or a wheelchair—that perhaps a stunt like that might properly convey my disability, might announce my pain in a way that made people understand that I was not alright. That they should not expect me to be alright. That I might not ever be. That reducing me to someone who "looks amazing" (goddamn right I do) so that they could squirm away from their own discomfort was a disservice to us both.

I did get married eventually. But I was too sick to be married. My sweet husband was a lovely, innocent human who got just as fucked by my illness as I did. I was not the person he had wanted to marry. I was a husk. My doctors advised that I'd have to wait at least three years to try for children; my body could simply not support or survive a pregnancy. We didn't make it past a year, and it wasn't his fault. I'm grateful we're still friends.

But still, I am one of the lucky ones. I actually *am* OK. It took many years to regain my footing as a functional human, and I'm still finding it. When your vocabulary is reduced to a third-grade level and you have to learn to use a pen again and there are things that you just cannot remember because they lived in the part of your brain that was destroyed, you need a fucking minute to regroup. But regroup I have.

I play word games now to keep myself sharp; my memory is not what it once was and may not ever be, but it's good enough. (I am also old as fuck and likely senile-adjacent.) I exercise and do sports to remind myself that I am in a living body and that it can do things now that I was certainly not promised when the Lyme was raging. Hell, I'm just getting out of bed every day, and THAT makes me lucky.

And not to be too clichéd about it all—because you know I'm not here for the triumph-of-the-human-spirit bullshit—but Lyme actually gave me many gifts, the best of which is extreme empathy for others who might look OK but are not. Patience for people who are struggling. Benefit of the doubt. A little fucking grace to spare.

Don't underestimate the impact your compassion can have on someone who needs it. I'm grateful that I can give that compassion with my whole heart. Because I get it, and I'm not sure I would have if not for Lyme. So yeah, I'm actually grateful for it. Grateful to be able to truly listen to someone or to take their hand and simply say, "That must be hard." Or "I'm really sorry you're going through that."

Or better yet?

"I believe you."

There's magic in those words. We all deserve to hear them.

4 / madness is an honest business

Admit it—you know you're weird, and you know it's *someone's* fault. And while it is tempting (and sometimes necessary) to point judgy, bitter fingers at our childhood caretakers, I'm a steadfast proponent of strapping on our Big Girl, um, strap-ons, sacking up, and taking responsibility for our own adult shit. With that said, we all come from somewhere, and we all come by our personal madness honestly. No one escapes the peripheral damage of a family on fire. Our only hope is to treat the burns and get the fuck out of the house (preferably draped over the sculpted shoulder of a beefy firefighter, who—oh, dear—seems to have lost his shirt in the fracas).

My family was an inferno, with my mother starring as the head arsonist in charge.

She was, to put it kindly, a piece of work. To put it less kindly, she was absolutely bonkers. Bat-shit crazy. And in fairness, she came by *her* crazy honestly, too. Her only crime was not acknowledging that she needed help, and instead letting her mental illness become the loudest voice and most formidable force in our family.

She was scarily brilliant, profoundly kind, and generous to a fault—I confess I don't talk enough about the good parts of my mom, and there were plenty of good parts. She loved fiercely. She rescued countless animals and went to the metaphorical ends of the earth to help folks in need. She purchased computers and cars for near-strangers to help them enter the job market; she paid for her employees' children to attend private schools and expensive colleges. Her generosity was legendary. Indeed, her good qualities were plentiful. But they were most often no match for the monsters. My mother could (and did, always) flip on a dime between tenderness and terrorist with no warning. To be honest, those moments of pure kindness made what inevitably came next even worse. With each unforeseen emotional Hiroshima came not only the fear and shame you might expect, but also a profound sense of betrayal. She tricked you into letting your guard down. You knew better and you did it anyway. Regardless, some of the shit she pulled was hilarious. Her anxieties drove her to behavior so outlandish, I have no choice but to record it for posterity. And for my therapist.

The primary lesson I learned as a child was that whatever was troubling, bothering, aching, ailing, or itching me was Probably Cancer. My moles and freckles were mapped and inventoried on a regular basis, and my mother's display of laden dread at the appearance of a new one was always Oscar-worthy.

"Oh my god," she'd whimper-whisper, her face crumpling into folds of resigned anguish. The inevitable childhood freckle cancer was *happening now*. "Oh my god."

Poops were checked for texture and timeliness, form and frequency. Temperatures were taken on the sly with the seemingly innocent brush of hand against forehead. Swollen glands, headaches, fatigue—no matter how occasional—were all indisputable proof that death was coming at me from all angles as my mother kept vigilant watch, using her extensive medical reference library as both a shield and a weapon, the clear message being "You need me. Without me protecting you, you will die. And it will hurt like a mofo."

This was enough to keep me poised in a state of quiet, obedient horror for much of my childhood. And by "childhood," I mean "until sometime last Thursday."

Theoretically, this could have been something of a burden on a young lass. But not me. While other, less informed children were sniffling over their everyday boo-boos, I was expressing my sincere concern over the possibility (probability, let's face it) that those little playground tumbles and gym-glass collisions—brought on, obviously, by rare but deadly pediatric TIAs (look it up, folks)—would result in a spate of fatal subdural hematomata that the school nurse never saw coming.

"Don't fall asleep," I told them, with great eight-year-old authority. "That brain bleed will kill you."

They didn't listen, of course. Idiots. They'd all be dead by morning.

I was instructed to be always on the lookout for "hard, pea-sized lumps" in my breasts (which I was years away from sprouting) or anywhere, really. Cancer liked to party in *allll* the body parts, she assured me. The trick was finding it early. I didn't want to end up like our neighbor, Mr. Johnson, who lost his entire nose to melanoma, did I?

NO, I DID FUCKING NOT. That shit was terrifying.

As I grew older, the threats mounted, obviously. Bicycles, cars, sports, air travel, choking, strangers, rogue tidal waves, errant space debris, "mashers" (to this day, I've never heard anyone else use this word, but I consider it a classic nonetheless) all lay in wait, coiled and ready to strike. Only hypervigilance would save me. And my mother.

My college years were defined by the five-times-weekly

greeting cards I received from her—much to the envy of my friends and roommates. See, the cards all contained $5 bills—ostensibly lunch money, but more often than not used to buy Camel Lights and Grateful Dead decals for my car—tucked, always, inside a current news clipping about the gruesome demise of some unsuspecting (aka disobedient) co-ed who made the mistake of leaving the house, ever.

Detailed accounts of chopped-up lady-pieces, kidnapping victims turned to skin-suits, severed limbs from careless car-waving peppered my daily intake of information and education. I came to understand that the $5 bills were little daily bribes to Not Do whatever activity led to that day's featured atrocity.

A little more of her madness osmosed itself into my head each day, and it sometimes worked. My college years were tragically tame as a result. Minimal drinking, zero drugs, zero sex. The sex part wasn't my mom's fault—I was just way too weird and awkward for anyone to wanna hit that. The harder I tried to be cool and attractive, the more certainly I'd fall over, shit my pants, or light my hair on fire (while wishing the hair flames would just engulf me whole and finish the job).

Like the time I trotted across campus in my tennis togs, heading for practice with my enormous racquet bag slung over my shoulder, exuding an effortless, athletic confidence, I was sure—until I tripped on the pavement in the middle of the bustling quad and landed in a perfect face-down X formation, surrounded by a dozen escaped tennis balls and quite a bit of blood. This moment lives in my head as a literal crime scene, with the chalk body outline drawn around the murdered corpse of my chance at ever getting laid in college. But I digress.

After graduation, I returned to my hometown and sooner than later got my own place. My comings and goings were, of course, closely monitored by my mother on what she called her nightly "rounds" (New Jersey state law, oddly enough, calls it "stalking").

Every night around eleven, I would see the headlights slowly approach my dwelling and come to a meaningful stop. My mother would then make some sort of ingenious thirty-seven-point turn in a triumphant maneuver designed to bright-light every inch of the front and sides of my house—most notably the bushes lined up wholesomely beneath my front windows (evidently a favorite hiding spot for lurking mashers).

When my property was scrutinized to her satisfaction, she would quietly drive away, only to return the next night, and the next. If, by some miracle, I was not at home during "rounds," she would simply wait for my return ... at which time, she and her headlights would silently illuminate my way, ensuring that I was not bludgeoned to death on my short journey from driveway to doorstep.

On one particularly perilous winter day during graduate school, my mother called me crying—a sure sign that some crafty plot was afoot.

"Please," she begged, "don't go to school today. *It's too dangerous!"*

I told her firmly that I had an exam and that the matter was not up for discussion—I would wear my seat belt and drive very slowly, but I was GOING to school.

The crying became more theatrical as she frantically asked if I still had my polo helmet (a remnant from one of the more useless life-enhancing skill sets I was forced to acquire as a privileged child), which she "strongly suggested" I wear for protection while walking across the snowy campus if I insisted upon disobeying her. (Did I mention graduate school?)

As I snidely assured her that I would not be wearing a polo

helmet to the college campus, her hysteria reached a feverish new cant—culminating in a high-pitched, frantic command to fetch my colander from the kitchen and affix it to my head with some shoelaces or fancy gift-wrap ribbon.

I shit you not, my friend. I shit you not. You laugh, but this was my life, and it was getting worse.

The bright spot in the Tale of the Lifesaving Colander is that somehow, this particular benchmark of my parental anti-neglect evolved into a totally awesome and legendary drinking game called, obviously, Colander Head. Similar in nature to Telephone, the last player to fumble the sequence was forced to wear the colander while the rest of us drank from our Solo cups and chanted, "Colander head, colander head! What the fuck is a colander head?"

When I was struck by an actual real-life illness, you can imagine that her fixation upon my imminent death became even more pronounced. And despite her expert surveillance, my mother would routinely become convinced that I was dead at the bottom of my own staircase if I did not return her calls in a timely manner. These fits would usually end with her breaking into and entering my home in search of my crumpled corpse, inevitably setting off the alarm system, which I obtained for this reason alone.

The day I knew for sure that I had to move away was the day my mother's break-in resulted in the entire police AND fire departments of my small, small town responding to the call and traipsing through my home, radios crackling and weapons at the ready. Alas, they did not find any cagey intruders or my rotting, fileted remains—but they DID find the *Playgirl* magazine (opened to centerfold), sequined pasties, penis straws, and chain-mail thong I had purchased for a friend's upcoming bachelorette, sitting shiny-and-new on my kitchen counter. It was the Brad Pitt issue. You would've looked, too.

You may be wondering where the rest of my family fits into this grim fable, and the sad truth is that they mostly don't. While technically one of three, I was virtually an only child. My much-older brothers were, wisely, long gone and not around to temper the storms or ensure equitable distribution of my mother's crushing dominance.

They'd moved far out of reach of her nightly rounds and home break-ins, and were fairly unscathed by my mother's ever-intensifying mental illness. When they were young, she was barely eccentric; her age and continued life let-downs ensured that her untreated madness continued to escalate. Lucky me.

My father, a good-natured dude for the most part, did not partake in any of the menacing death-peddling himself, but was powerless to rein my mother in and decisively punished whenever he tried. My dad's relative sanity was no match for my mom's spectacular lunacy.

He was a bright light of regular-dad energy in my young life, and I felt safe with him. It was Dad that I turned to when preteen acne began hiding beneath my Dorothy Hamill bangs in middle school; he simply took my hand and drove me to the drugstore for some Stri-Dex pads and told me it would be better in a few days. Can you imagine my mother's display of narcissistic stagecraft in this situation?

"Oh my god," she'd have wheezed, frantically. "That's meningococcal meningitis. *We're all doomed.*"

My father's spirit quietly died sometime in my teen years and he became angry and disengaged. Not the present, light-hearted father that had come to my peewee softball games and taken me to Indian Princesses once a month. (I am cringing at this, of course: a horrifying and insensitive appropriation. Nonetheless, some of my sweetest memories were made there with my dad, in our homemade feather headdresses with all the other little white girls and their well-meaning white fathers. UGH.)

He had checked out, and I cannot blame him. I don't know how he stayed at all. But as I got a little older, I became afraid of his well-earned temper and we grew apart. Still, any sense of grounding or normalcy in my life came from him, and I loved him for that.

Missy, my childhood nanny, did her best to shield me from the worst of the bullshit going on with the adults, but her reach could only extend so far. She often took the blame for me when I failed my mother's never-ending perfect-child obstacle course of music/dance/sports practice, error-free homework, and Emily Post porn. Missy was unfailingly kind, and helped me through things (like menstruation) that my mother wouldn't touch with a ten-foot polo mallet. But still. They were small mercies hidden in a very large pile of shit.

My parents split up eventually, which only served to make my mother's grip on me even tighter and more intractable. I took it as long as I could, but after the infamous *Playgirl* incident, it was time, I knew. I had to go.

And go I did. Far, far away and never to return. And though I loved my mother dearly and truly ached for her burdens, they were no longer my burdens. I had to see if there was any life for me outside of her reach. So, my friend, while we take a moment and together marvel at my own relative sanity, there's just one last thing. To the rented-kitchen-full of over-privileged twenty-somethings enjoying a raucous round of Colander Head somewhere on the Jersey shore at this very moment: *You're welcome, bitches.*

5 / sex and the shitty

It probably won't surprise you to learn that I've been single, off and on, for most of my life. Despite my delightful demeanor (That's right. Delightful.), most dudes have historically been (a) exquisitely uncomfortable in the presence of my awkwardness, or (b) absolutely terrified that I'd "rip their balls off" if they screwed it up. That's a direct quote from a crush who did not return my pants-feelings. And to be honest, both reactions to my amorous advances are hella valid.

For the purpose of disclosure, I am, according to several of my gay friends, "tragically straight." And I feeeeel that, sister. I like to think I'd have better luck with the ladies, but I've never been able to get my ladybrain or my ladybits on board with trying. I'm hopelessly hetero.

I've always envied the gals who could effortlessly flirt with men or women they were interested in. Even the ones who could act remotely normal in front of the objects of their desire are basically my heroes. I'd have settled for that in a heartbeat. If a guy had the great misfortune of catching my eye anytime between 1982 and, say, yesterday, they were undoubtedly treated to a mortifying courtship display that left everyone involved embarrassed, frightened, and probably bleeding.

My attempts at seduction usually featured stress hives, jump-scare outbursts, terrible artwork, gastric emergencies, tragic poetry, and always, always, accidental tripping, falling, burping, spilling, snorting, dribbling, snot-rockets, and generalized physical malfunctions.

My paltry self-esteem combined with the Victorian-era avoidance of any remotely real, personal, social, or emotional discourse in my family home left me absolutely ill-prepared to be anyone's crush. At all. Or to express my own crushes in a civilized manner.

There were occasionally boys who found my romantic incompetence endearing, or who bonded with me over a shared love of fart jokes or Christopher Guest movies. But generally speaking, anyone who eventually became my boyfriend had a LOT of layers of emotional and physical pandemonium to conquer to get to my gooey center. And it wasn't always worth it. To those intrepid souls: I salute you. Your bravery is commendable.

My first husband, the bravest of them all, was actually a lovely, kind boy who was simply and unexpectedly in over his head. For most of the 358 days we were married, I was either in bed, the hospital, or a Vicodin haze as I navigated my new life with Lyme disease. Poor kiddo. Sickness and health was not supposed to be NOW. He tried, he really did.

He was awfully kind when he was home with me—he was just very rarely home with me. He needed time away from the House of Doom and Gloom, which I understand much better now than I did at the time (for that is where I grew up; what's wrong with a little misery and madness, I wondered?). But the fact remained that while his teenage-y social life raged on like a prom-night kegger, I was at home dying.

The paralysis, memory loss, and excruciating pain of my illness did not make me a very understanding wife, I'm afraid, and I started to leave in my mind long before my body could muster the strength to do it. With no hope for babies anytime soon, I simply checked out.

Then 9/11 happened, and as I watched my friends disintegrate and rain from the sky on live television, it all became very clear. This marriage wasn't what I wanted and it also wasn't fair to him. We could not take care of each other the way we had hoped. It took me another month to cut the cord—funerals and memorials and vigils filled the days and weeks that followed. Then, nothing. And I left.

This is all I have ever written or likely ever will write about 9/11. There simply aren't words for what it was like to watch those buildings across the river burn *for months,* to wait for news about missing bodies, to feel the fighter jets shake your literal foundation. I won't even try. Suffice it to say that it changed everything, forever. It broke relationships or it saved them. Mine broke.

I had only one actual relationship between husbands (the tale of Husband Number Two is an abomination unto itself, and I'll get there, I promise; you'll want to grab a drink or three), and that one was supposed to be *it.* We were star-crossed from moment one, and immediately began a gut-wrenching long-distance relationship that would ultimately lead us both to relocate in great dramatic fashion just to be together. This boy ignited my heart and stole my sleep and tangled my insides in a way that I had never felt before and certainly haven't since. It was love like you read about, and *I had to have it.*

The onnnnly problem was (which took me a year to figure out), my dude was a raging porn addict with serious mommy issues. He was eight years my junior, emotionally asphyxiated, and so, so broken. But I persevered! I loved him! I would see this through! We even looked forward to the day that he was "cured" so we could have T-shirts made up saying "I Had a Porn Addiction, and I Beat It." (All me, obviously. Here all week, folks.)

But then (then!) shit got weird. The soulless dolphin-flogging escalated and he spun out of control in every direction, exploding our life together like shrapnel and breaking everything he touched. (Everything except, well, *that.* That proved quite sturdy.)

He ultimately left me one morning two years later with the following announcement: "It's not me. It's you. I believe that you're not good enough for me and that I can do better."

Riiiiiiiiiight, buddy. Good luck with that.

I was still crushed. And I sort-of believed him.

After a suitable period spent wallowing in his lingering emotional toxins and disinfecting all of my keyboards, I reluctantly entered the Match.com Years. I know it has its virtues—I've seen the commercials! But for me it felt like plunging naked into a bubbling cauldron of lies, vanity, snakes, and someone else's diarrhea. I did it though—I HAD to, my friends said. They wanted me to be happy, they said. Mostly I think they saw the entertainment value in my inevitable suffering, but whatevs. I did it anyway.

My crusade to find Love, Millennium-Style, led me through the war-torn landscape of middle-aged starting-overs seeking "best friends," young'uns seeking MILFs, douchelords seeking models, and me, seeking someone who could spell. It also resulted in more grainy dick-pic emails from their proud owners than I can count. (Yes, email, the preferred medium for early-aughts penis-wielding asshats—who had to go to the trouble of scanning and uploading actual paper photographs of their penises, procured from unsuspecting One-Hour Photo shops before cellphone cameras streamlined their penis-bombing process.)

It may not be necessary to mention that this Romantic Jihad resulted in lots of first dates. And not one single second. It also, incidentally, resulted in the slow death of all my hopes and dreams. And a restraining order.

A sampling of my deviant suitors, for your enjoyment and in no particular order:

Tearful Todd, who cried at dinner and Only Ate Shrimp. Todd couldn't understand why I wouldn't "let him love me" and expressed concern during his shrimp appetizer that his striking resemblance to Keith Urban was hindering his search for true love. The "ladies" only seemed to want him for his good looks, he said, not his fathomless, dreamy soul. I explained that, indeed, I was probably one of those "ladies" and, apologizing, left him crying in his shrimp dinner. Check, please.

Earnest Ponytail Poetry Guy wrote me a "song" on a napkin that had been smudged with some kind of gravy, and handed it to me triumphantly, explaining that my beauty had "taken him somewhere" and the words just poured out of him like holy wine. I don't remember much about the song now except that it contained the phrase "elbow grease." Also, it contained actual grease. From the gravy. On the napkin.

Next came Joe, who offered up quite a refreshing package in comparison to most of my other one-dates. Handsome, charming, chatty, intelligent, even a little funny! Joe gave me hope that this was not my personal Armageddon, after all, and I thought, *Hmm—if HE asks me out again, I will say yes.* And ask he did—even offering up *another* package to sweeten the deal—this one significantly less refreshing. Indeed, somehow Joe's clammy junk ended up being thrust into my unsuspecting grip during a chaste hug-shake (you know, the awkward hug/handshake hybrid?), which has, to this very day, drastically altered my trust level when extending my hand to anyone, ever. I'll never un-feel Joe's junk. Like a ghost limb ... but with junk. Thanks for nothing, Ghost-Junk Joe.

For brevity's sake, I'll wrap things up with a list of the swains whose catchy monikers endured long past the horror of my twelve-ish minutes with each of them: Pretentious Tongue-Smacking Wine Snob; Doesn't Know He's Gay Yet; Guy Who Asked If He Might Borrow My Car Overnight; Forgot My Wallet(s) 1–7; Stalker Stephan (pronounced Stef-ON); One-Tooth; Sir "Does the Carpet Match the Drapes?"; and a gentleman known simply as "Backne."

There were others, dear friends, most of whom never made it to the first date due to calamitous grammar crimes or aforementioned peen-mail. Oh, yes, there were others. However, high upon the Royal Float in my parade of stunning romantic flame-outs sits a fellow who will forever be known, triumphantly, to me and my trusty confidantes, as Taco Toe. Yes, he did exactly what it sounds like he did. And no, I did not see it coming. He was very limber. And had spectacular aim.

Dating is a horrifying business. Soul-crushing, junk-thrusting devilry. And for what? Some Cinderella shit that doesn't even exist? I mean, when a relationship "works out," we're basically just signing up for long-term soul-crushing and junk-thrusting, aren't we? Along with eternal floor-underwear, remote control wars, overflowing garbage cans, dirty dishes, and pubes EVERYWHERE.

But I may be a little jaded.

A big toe to the vadge will do that to a girl.

6 / marketable skills (and other things i don't have, according to my mother)

I've spent a lonnng time trying to figure out exactly why I'm so fucked-up, and I think the problem is that I'm so fucked-up in so many areas, it's hard to choose one and pin down The Reason. Each individual fiefdom of my fucked-upedness has its own feudal lord pulling the fucked-up strings. Most often, it's my mother. Go figure.

She was the kindest and most deeply good, moral, and empathetic person I've ever known. She was also, at times, a monster. That is the truth and it's the thing that has made untangling my own demons so very difficult. An impossible dichotomy. I loved my mom and I wanted her to love me—which she did, fiercely.

She also conflated love with her own paralyzing anxiety, which she could not name but which was piloting the emotional Hindenburg of her influence 100 percent of the time. She was consumed by the danger of life and certain that if she let her guard down for even one minute, something awful would happen to me. "Protecting" me was the fire that fueled her existence, and she called that love. I called it martial law.

She mistook control for love, exerting her iron will to mold and shape me into the version of myself that caused her the least amount of pain. She kept me close and she kept me scared, which kept me safe. Mission accomplished.

This created a stunted reality in which I was not encouraged—not allowed, even—to try. Anything. Sometimes I marvel that my mom let me do gymnastics and play tennis and softball as a kid, and it makes sense only because she was simply not as ill back then. She got worse and worse as her life went on; her anxiety fed on itself and it drove her further to the brink each year.

She violently opposed anyone's suggestion that she needed help; any such affront ended with that ~~lucky bastard~~ person being permanently removed from her life, and eventually there was no one left to say it. No one dared.

She had no joy of her own. She hated my father, she hated herself, she hated everything about her life except her children. My brothers got off pretty easy here, at least as kids. My oldest brother recently shared a memory with me that blew my goddamn mind: My mother used to have dance parties with my brothers when they were small, doing the twist in the living room to Beatles records.

HUH???

How did they have a completely different childhood than I did? A completely different mom? They were simply gone and out of the house before things got awful. I got the awful. The Overlord. The Prison Guard. The Love Terrorist.

I know she tried to pull the same shit with my brothers as adults, but it never took. They were never as susceptible to her dominance as I was, but fuck if she didn't try. She regaled us all with tales of murder and mayhem—remember the news clippings? The colander? The helmet? Bitch did not play. If she thought there was a way to successfully keep us all locked in her basement, she would have tried it. But because Social

Services are a thing, our locked basement was merely metaphorical, but no less damaging.

However, I alone drank the Kool-Aid. Her fear became my fear. Her ever-present dread quietly slipped into my own subconscious, where her tricks and manipulations found easy purchase.

So when, after college, I had two enviable job offers that would have required me to commute to NYC each day, she shut that shit down, stat. City meant danger. Danger meant death. Unable to express her fears in a vulnerable or self-aware way, she went in a different direction.

"Oh, honey. You're not ... nine-to-five material."

Subtext: *I was lazy. I was naïve. I wasn't good at anything. I was weird. I would fail. They'd eat me alive. I'd be better off staying home with her. She'd take care of me.*

She was right. Who was I kidding?

I turned them down. Both offers, right then.

Cue thirty fucking years of soul-smashing regret.

So, for years I stayed in my hometown, chronically underemployed at small retail and tutoring jobs—if I worked at all. My mother kept me contented (or so she thought) with expensive gifts and shopping trips—my therapist calls this the Golden Handcuff syndrome and fuck ME if that isn't the most accurate shit I've ever heard. Though I lived on my own, my mother was never far from the scene—making her nightly rounds and breaking into my house whenever she'd convinced herself I was dead in a heap at the bottom of the stairs.

From time to time, I'd hear about a job or opportunity that got me excited about trying for something more, and my mother's response was always the same: "Oh, honey. You have no ... marketable skills."

She's right. I suck at everything. What even is the point of me? I am nothing and no one.

The one thing my mother never talked me out of—she didn't even try—was volunteering at a bird rehabilitation center down in the swamplands of NJ (cuz wrangling enraged eagles isn't dangerous AT ALL), about an hour from my hometown. I'd fallen in love—despite my pre-existing abject terror of birds—with a baby cardinal I found abandoned, and nursed it until I'd located a place that would take him in and care for him properly. I couldn't bear to part with him, but I knew it would be unkind to keep him.

So I boxed my little bird up, buckled us in, and listened to Sarah McLachlan's "I Will Remember You" on repeat the whole way down to the center. (Why do I do this to myself, you ask? Fuck if I know.) I was in such inconsolable hysterics when I dropped off my bird baby that one of the kind-hearted volunteers ran after me to say that I could visit him anytime, and be there when they released him back into nature if I wanted. He also said they were looking for volunteers, and that I should think about it.

I didn't need to think about it. My bird fear had evaporated, whiplash-like, and I was all in. But I *did* need to ask my mom. I was only thirty, for fuckssake.

Through my work at the Raptor Trust, my already irrational love for animals grew exponentially. I had always preferred the company of my dogs and cats, as well as the horses, goats, sheep, and chickens that I'd grown up with on my parents' and grandpa's farms. Humans were awful; hateful and hard. Animals were easy and uncomplicated: I loved them and they loved me back without all the confusing conditions and emotional waterboarding that people seemed to enjoy. I had an almost supernatural gratitude for the Raptor Trust—for the peace and purpose I'd found there. *Holy fuck, I had a purpose.* I worked there for years, and it was absolutely magical.

It got me thinking about going to vet school, and whether, in my thirties, it was too late. Probably it was. But maybe not?

Not too long after I'd first found my refuge at the Raptor Trust, I got an out-of-the-blue phone call from the minister at my family's church. This is probably obvious, but I am not a believer or churchgoer. *Like, at alllllll.* If there was a religion for foul-mouthed, Pagan-adjacent berserkers (I mean, is there? I want IN), that was what I was. But I did have a really nice friendship with this gentleman—he was cool and rational, and had been an English major/heathen in college like I had. He was later called to the church, but retained his ability to think critically despite his strong faith.

We had some awesome talks back in the day. He knew where I stood and didn't try to change my mind, ever. We just talked about literature, loss, poetry, and purpose. Plus, he looked like Santa Claus, and Santa is fucking awesome.

I was taken by surprise when his call came, because we hadn't talked or seen each other in a couple of years. *Probably someone is dead,* I thought, most Mom-like. But nobody was dead. He was calling to tell me something that he wasn't sure I'd believe but that he had to tell me anyway. He'd had a visit from the Big Guy. Il Capo. El Queso Grande. It wasn't something that happened to him often, he assured me, but when it did happen, he felt it was his duty to report it.

He'd gotten a very clear message from God—right outta nowhere—that I, Marie, had a purpose in this earthly life and that purpose was to work with animals. To heal and help them. He said God made it sound very important. Urgent, even. Did any of this make sense to me? he wanted to know.

Wait. Holy shit. God knows about me? Well, I am most certainly FUCKED.

Then came the goose bumps—and the tears.

"Are you shitting me? I've been thinking about this exact.

same. thing. myself. Are you fucking with me, Padre? Am I on *Candid Camera?*"

He assured me that he was neither fucking with nor filming me, and that he was simply the middle man. He hung up and of course—because, evidently, I am a glutton for punishment (and a colossal, man-size idiot)—I immediately called my mother to tell her this incredible tale. About God. And vet school.

"Oh, honey. Vet school is ... hard."

And that was it. Four words that leveled me. Put me forever in my place. Reduced to ashes.

I am nothing. I am no one.

Spoiler alert: I did not go to vet school. I did not give it another thought. My mother was the almighty authority, not God. What the fuck did God know?

Sometimes, now, I marvel at the brass goddamn balls on her. Like, for real. God himself basically slid into my DMs to tell me to be a vet, and my mother's like "Nah." Jesus Fucking Christ.

Why did I listen to her? you are wondering. While that's a really excellent question, surely it must be obvious: Because I believed her.

I believed her.

While I will never fully know why I willingly took it so hard up the ass from my mother time and time again, I do now understand (after approximately two hundred years of therapy) what compelled *her* to cut me into ribbons at the first whispered hint of evolution. It was Fear, that seven-headed murder monster that lived inside her and made her say awful things to keep me safe. By any means necessary. Convincing me I wasn't good for much except being her not-dead daughter was her chosen strategy, and it worked like a fucked-up charm.

Of course, I grieve the life I could have had and wonder,

always, where all those ultimately impotent ideas about my future would have led me had I been encouraged instead of crushed. But the truth is that she lives inside me still. I share her anxieties, and while I am much better at managing them (thank you, Big Pharma!), you'd better believe I hear that "Oh, honey" in my head on the regular. Still.

Now, when I hear it, I just say, "Hi, Mom. Fuck off. I've got this." And I do the damn thing.

I *can* do hard things. I have done hard things. I'm kind of a badass, to be absolutely fucking honest. I own my choices, the occasional good ones and especially the shitty ones. I do what I want and what I love, and I am good at it. I am getting braver all the time, despite my every inclination to not be.

I fight the "Oh, honeys" in my head and I win. Mostly.

It's a daily battle and I'm damn lucky to be alive to fight it, what with all the working and driving and learning and going outside to get the mail that I do now. I'd like to believe that she could be proud of me for being strong and stubborn enough to subvert her will to save my soul. But I'm not an idiot. I'm not a fool.

Nor am I a vet.

I have no current intel on how God feels about all this. Fucking guy never takes my calls. It's weird.

7 / my dog is a jerk

THIS IS WELL documented. Astronomical vet bills (mostly of the emergent *removal* nature, by various means), Petco receipts for designer food and increasingly barbarous contraptions for bark control, failing grades in behavior school, and even a visiting pet psychic (diagnosis: "Hilarious." WTF?) tell the tale better than I can.

But I shall try, for your amusement, my friend—and to boost your self-esteem. For whatever shortcomings you may assign yourself, I can assure you that my pet-rearing miscarriages make your failures and inadequacies look Nobel Prize–worthy.

Bucky. This is the name of my canine vexation. Named, obviously, for the dishy Yankees shortstop who stole both my heart and the World Series in 1978, Bucky Fuckin' Dent is truly the bane of my existence. Just a terrible goddamn dog.

Problem is, like most cankers upon the cheek-meat of womankind, he is also adorable. Twinkly, deep-brown eyes, explosions of whisper-soft yellow fluff, an earflap-to-earflap smile worthy of an old-timey Gleem commercial, full-body joy wagging, and the most endearing tendency to drop to his back and pee straight into the air in helpless elation upon my arrival home from even the briefest of errands—like, say, retrieving the mail from outside—are all components of his Cuteness Kryptonite. Resistance is futile.

A brief rundown of his signature infractions:

1. Several times per night, Bucky emits a high-pitched, closed-mouth, sonar-like squeaking that only I can hear. This particular brain dagger can mean one or more of the following: He is tired, but not asleep; he is asleep and having a bad dream; he has to pee; he has to poop; he has diarrhea (again); he is hungry (again); he is bored; he is hot; he is cold; he would please like to snuggle. Since the whining will not stop until I have addressed his demands, I am perpetually sleep-deprived and wearing the glazed-over countenance usually reserved for new mothers and post-apocalyptic zombie-folk. Only without the smashing knockers and/or license to feast upon my enemies. It pretty much sucks.
2. Then there's the barking. Dear God, the barking. If the military torture honchos ever succumb to demands for less "ethically casual" means of inflicting exquisite agony upon our prisoners of war, I will proudly do my patriotic duty and lend them my dog. The searing, unendurable, and constant vocal bedlam is the emotional equivalent of a violent fence-post impalement that you are forced to survive despite your devout and fevered begging for God to kill you.
3. Eating things that should not be eaten, ever, is another Bucky forte. He routinely parades freshly found bone fragments of ill-fated woodland

creatures around like a haughty showgirl before ingesting them as I watch, frozen in horror. Oozing dead things are an obvious favorite. (Did you know that, by some alchemical magic, desiccated lizard carcasses—like peas—somehow reconstitute when commingled with the other key ingredients in vomit? True story.) Cat shit, birdseed, glass, rocks, used underpants, and feminine products—all on the menu and all acquired by illegal means such as counter-surfing and hamper-diving. Luckily, my larger-and-in-charger dog, Karma, can get him to drop almost any of the offending snack choices he's toting (today, horse poo) and hang his head in shame with one withering, judgmental glare. I have taught her well.

4. However, sadly, not even she can discourage the incessant, desperate dry-humping—she (and I) can only watch impotently as he unsheathes the pink lipstick, approaches his target slowly, and erupts into the frenzied thrashing of a pimply teen virgin in a Tijuana whorehouse. It's a little embarrassing.

The result of all this is that I spend much (most) of every day thinking of ways to outsmart, correct, or misplace him, and failing miserably. I've considered donating him to science, but science doesn't deserve that. Therefore, I am perpetually beleaguered; resigned to defeat and shame for the next fifteen or so years of my "nobody-will-ever-love-me-because-of-my-horrible-dog" life.

But then, come bedtime, when he smells like Fritos and sunshine and falls asleep smiling, tongue out with his head on my chest while he gazes at me adoringly, I snuggle into the comforting cushion of banana fluff and know, with certainty, that I will do it all again tomorrow. Gladly.

It is thirteen years since I wrote the above confession, and Bucky is still with me. He also happens to be, now, the Best Dog in the Whole World. He is nearly fifteen, and, finally, at the top of the food chain in the current hierarchy of my pets. He has earned his retirement.

He has arthritis now, just like the rest of us, and struggles with an old injury he sustained when my awful second husband hit him with his car "accidentally." He creaks and limps and does his best to climb up on the couch for his signature snuggles. I've put down nonslip flooring in all his favorite spots so his old-man legs don't splay out beneath him. It's unbearable to see him struggle. I make him bone broth for his joints and give him CBD oil for inflammation and medication for his pain.

Somehow, during Covid, my front lawn became ground zero for socially distant gatherings when the isolation started getting to everyone. Every Friday night, friends and neighbors would safely convene outside my house, and Bucky was the only one of my dogs who was well-behaved enough to join us. He was the star of the show, of course, and relished his role as guest of honor. He pretty quickly started knowing when it was Friday, and would spend all day in fits of delight, just knowing he was gonna get to party with his people friends. Dude loves to party.

These days, Bucky needs help in and out of the car, but it still gives him unfathomable joy to "go for a ride" with his mamma. I take him to hydrotherapy for his weak legs and to the chiropractor for his aging frame, and we always stop for ice cream after his appointments. What's the harm now?

I am not deluding myself. I know his time is limited and that no amount of designer veterinary care can make him stay forever. My heart knows it will be terribly broken someday soon. He's been with me through the worst of everything, even when the worst of everything was him.

It doesn't seem possible that he's the same dog that vexed me so. My Bucky now is perfect. And he's truly been living his best life. No regrets.

While I dread the day I will have to say goodbye, I am profoundly grateful for the time we've had together and the time we still have ahead of us, even if it is short. I make every day we have as sweet and special as I possibly can.

Each night before bed, I rub his head and kiss his soft ears and tell him all the things I love about him. As he smiles at me and gazes up at me adoringly, I thank him for being my best pal. For letting me be his mom. I tell him that every day together is the best day ever.

His life has been a gift, even at his hilarious worst. It's also been a lesson: to not give up on those we love, even when they're not particularly lovable. To not focus so fiercely on the bad things that you miss out on the good things. To occasionally overlook the lipstick and the lizard barf in order to find the soft, sleepy snuggles they might be obscuring. To have some faith and patience—neither of which is my forte—that maybe the terrible will be temporary.

I ask Bucky each night to let me know when it's time, so I don't make him stay any longer than he wants to. And when that day comes, through my awful tears, I will tell him that it's only goodbye for now, not goodbye forever. And I will hope like hell that it's the truth.

And I'll tell him that he's been the very best boy, because that *is* the truth.

8 / "i'm not saying that"

I DO NOT want to write this chapter. I am getting stabby just thinking about it. But it's rather crucial that you know this part of my saga, so here you go, fuckers. I'm doing this for you.

When I left NJ to recover from Lyme disease and, um, my mother, I chose Park City, Utah, primarily because it was really, really far away; but it was also the exact right climate for me while I was convalescing. Dry and cold. I felt physically amazing there for the first time in years and, more compelling still, it was incredibly liberating to live someplace where I wasn't being stalked in my own home by, shall we say, over-interested parties. That, my friend, would not last long.

DRAMATIC FORESHADOWING

I met the unrivaled ass-clown that would destroy my life (and become my second husband) about a year after I moved to Park City. A dear friend convinced me to give him a chance despite my truly icky first impression: smarmy, desperate, and shady as fuck. She reminded me that I hated literally everyone and that maybe this was a *me* problem, not a *him* problem.

When I finally agreed to a date, I spent the whole day trying to injure myself so I'd end up in urgent care and get to cancel. (I'm not kidding. I do this.) There was a new episode of the *OC* on that night and all I wanted to do, with the whole of my soul, was stay home and watch it alone.

I did not succeed in physically maiming myself, so I went. You may be wondering why I didn't just say I wasn't interested and not go on the date with the dude who made my skin crawl. I may have been wondering this for the past nineteen years as well.

I met him at the restaurant; I knew in my very bones that I did not want this fucker to know where I lived. He was late, and I kept asking the bartender how long I had to wait before I could leave; I was just about to, gleefully, when he finally showed up. Fuck. He was sweating profusely and confessed that he was incredibly nervous, which I found rather endearing, actually. Not what I expected. That was the moment he figured me out. I was unaware that he'd also been "researching" me online—which most people didn't even know how to do in 2005—so I was pleasantly surprised by all that we "had in common." I agreed to see him again. Dumbfuck.

He had always been prone to pompous bloviating in addition to the unfortunate stalking predilection: He told me early on that he was "getting a PhD," only to reveal later that he hadn't even finished his undergraduate degree. He tried to impress me with his knowledge of fine art and his own "collection," which I eventually found out had been pilfered from the gallery where he worked occasionally. He said that he was owed money. Ever guiltless.

I didn't give a shit about any of the things he was bragging about, and I must have made that clear. I did not yet know that he was a pathological liar, or that he was using my reaction to his showboating to map out the persona he was crafting: Someone I'd Like to Date. He took his cues and morphed himself into a semblance of boyfriend material.

He was in the middle of a very nasty divorce from a very

nasty woman when we met—another red flag I chose to ignore.

Oh yeah, and he had this kid, he said. I was gonna love him, he said.

I did not love said kid. He was awful. They were awful together, far worse than the sum of their parts.

Our dating relationship was fraught with drama: The ex-wife was hostile, alcoholic, and psychotic, calling me every version of fat and ugly she could think of on repeat. Ooooh, sick burn, dude. *eyeroll* She encouraged the child to also call me names, and when they referenced me to each other, I was "the Cow."

No one knew why I stayed. He was perpetually unemployed, broke, and "borrowing" my money. He lied relentlessly, even about stuff there was no reason to lie about. My mother loathed him, obviously—he was a ticking time bomb in her opinion, which I explained away by reminding myself that she had her own very focused agenda when it came to me and my life choices. My friends and nieces did not like him either; today, this alone would be the absolute deal-breaker. But in 2005, you know what else was ticking? My fucking biological clock. I was thirty-six. It was likely this guy or no one. He told me—always—he was on board for babies.

I lived through another couple years of this particular hell, with my eyes on the diaper-clad prize. It sounds INANE as I write this now. Why did I think having a baby with this manipulative, borderline-personality asswipe and his oppositional-defiance-disorder-asswipe child was a good idea? I can only blame my ovaries, which, as far as they were concerned, had *one fucking job.*

Our wedding was a lavish affair (he reeeealllly enjoyed spending my mother's money) at the Carlyle Hotel in NYC. That was for the benefit of my 104-year-old grandmother, who used to go to the Carlyle with my grandpa on Friday nights a million years ago to see Bobby Short play in Bemelmans Bar. We knew it would be her last outing before she died, and getting married in NY would save a lot of people a lot of trouble, as we were both East Coasters.

During the wedding rehearsal, our officiant led us through the ceremony and at one point she said, "OK, dickhole [she obviously didn't say exactly that, but this is MY book, motherfuckers], this is the part where you'll take Marie's hand and tell her that from now on, you will put her before everyone else; that all other relationships are secondary to the marital bond, and that you pledge to be a husband first and everything else second."

"I'm not saying that."

Huh?

"I'm not saying that. My kid will be sitting right there. I'm not saying it."

"But asswipe, sir, it's very important for him to hear that your marriage has to come first, so he understands that your primary relationship is with your wife."

"OK, well, I'll just talk to him first and tell him you're making me say it."

WHY DID I NOT RUN SCREAMING???

Because babies. And because my dress was FIRE, y'all. But I should have. I knew it. The officiant knew it. My mother obviously knew it, and she would have gladly forfeited the cost of the wedding if I'd made that choice. But I am a colossal fucking idiot. So I didn't.

Aside from my amazing dress, the most memorable thing about that day is that I saw Chris Cornell from Soundgarden walking through the lobby. He looked like the absolute smoking-hottest homeless guy in NYC. Which is saying something. But I digress.

Turdburger chose the honeymoon to tell me that he'd changed his mind about kids. That I already paid too much attention to my cats and dogs. If I had a baby, I'd have nothing left for him. End of discussion. I was stuck with an unemployed shitdick who really only wanted access to my checkbook.

A year or so later, my mother fell ill with a serious heart issue and needed surgery. I'd been wanting to move back home for a while—I loved Utah, but it was never going to be my real home, and we both spoke of making a clean start somewhere that the lunatic ex-wife hadn't poisoned yet—he said he could see that my mom's health situation was bad and that it would be best if I were back in NJ with the rest of my family and friends. He "agreed" to move back east (this was contingent upon me buying him a very expensive car in return, naturally) and we started the house hunt.

Two weeks later it was *Nah, fam, we're moving to Michigan.* And we did.

I could go on and on about all the times he lied, how he spent over a year catfishing me by creating a fake Facebook profile while we were still married, how he stalked me after I finally left him, and faked a suicide attempt to get me to come back. How he wrote a letter to my very ill mother saying our divorce was her fault.

How he took my RV and left it unlocked in Salt Lake City with the keys inside, refusing to give me its location because I wouldn't see him. How every phone call cycled through "I love you, I can't live without you" to "You fucking selfish cunt" to "Oh my god, I'm so sorry, I didn't mean it, I cannot lose you." How he threatened the family of someone I briefly dated after it was all done. How he violated my protective order by emailing me to gloat about his new girlfriend, then hacked my account to delete the evidence. And on and on.

I could. But I won't. Because the second I realized that I didn't have to pick up those phone calls anymore and listen to him call me names and beg and cry and promise, berate and manipulate and blame me, the lights came back on in my brain and I was free.

The damage he did will never be undone, no matter how much time and therapy hours go by. I do not forgive him. I do not forgive myself. I hate him with the fire of a thousand burning suns and I will never not hate him. I hate him more than I have ever hated or will ever hate any other thing or person on this planet, and folks? I HATE EVERYTHING.

I am, of course, stronger and smarter now. Menopause will do that for a gal who wanted a baby so badly she sold her soul just for the possibility. I live a peaceful life far away from his toxic ass. I know who I am and what I'm worth. The damage he caused would have been irreparable if not for my fierce resolve —fueled by undiluted Jersey juice—to crush it. However, it (and he) is filed in my Eternal Enemies dossier along with Hitler, acorn squash, Donald Trump, and the lady who gave me a mullet in eighth grade. But I do not dwell on it. I do not think about him.

And after all these years, I can say this with my whole heart: *I wish him nothing but the worst.*

9 / it's like clue, but with turds

Everything sucks sometimes. I think we can all agree on that. Sometimes and for some people, things suck way harder and for much too long, and there's just no tiara that will fit that particular turd. Toxic-positivity peddlers would have you believe it's all in the way you look at it; I've read enough bullshit self-help literature to know this. The curse becomes the gift, turn that frown upside down, silverlining/brightside/blahblahblah. Bite me, bro. I got it.

I try to stay positive, I really do. For example, if I hadn't had such a miserable, lonely childhood, I wouldn't have turned out so goddamned hilarious and able to entertain you with my antics. If my husband hadn't been such a deranged, weapons-grade dickhole, I would never have memorized the *Top 10 Signs You're Married to a Lunatic Handbook*—and, let's face it, that shit comes in handy. If I hadn't sustained irreversible brain damage from a tiny bug bite, I would not be enjoying the lifetime privilege of being allowed to forget people's names. See? I'm so positive. I'm like a ray of fucking sunshine.

There's one thing, though, that no matter how hard I've tried, I simply haven't been able to transmutate, reframe or celebrate: Shit. It's all the goddamned shit. Every. Single. Day. Of my life.

Living with a four-legged horde and a flock of chickens has sharpened my cleaning skills and bolstered my arsenal of shit-fighting products to Armageddon-ready (my favorite proclaims, without irony, *For Pet AND People Accidents.* How convenient is THAT?). When the End Times are upon us and everyone else is wondering how on earth they're going to get that pesky shit stain out, I'll be smugly buffing away. Don't come crying to me, people.

Of course, it's not just shit. Six (six!) house pets are inclined to produce all manner of bodily expulsions. Nearly every day I discover something that results in either irate profanity or bewildered wonderment—*What fresh hell is this*? I might say, while examining some unidentifiable heap of maybe-ass-cache. Puke, pee, hairballs, blood, farts (I don't really have to clean up farts, granted, but sometimes it takes a while to get them out of the couch.)

I also *find* things (like the cleanly bitten half-a-mouse in my garage the other day, his tiny face frozen in forever-horror as what I presume to be Karma, my giant she-wolf and prize asshole, took a dainty bite of his lower torso and decided that particular treat was not worth her trouble—sorry, 'lil mouse bro) that I somehow know will show up later in one of the aforementioned media. I have begun to brace myself when I come down the stairs each morning, certain that some mucousy horror awaits my bare footfalls.

So here is where my peculiar genius rears its shit-stained head: I've begun to be able to predict, to a certain degree, where and what I might find, based on sounds heard in the night, wafting aromas, what is missing from the counter, or how many dead frogs/birds/chipmunks were pried from jaws the day before. It's bloody brilliant. I'm like the Hercule-fucking-Poirot of household biohazards. And that's when it hit me.

Poo Clue.

It's a game. Games are fun, right?

Aaaand there it is. Your goddamned silver lining. Now, when I awake each morning, instead of creeping dread and a quivering uvula, I greet the day wearing my thinking cap (in my mind, it has a propeller) and get down to the business of solving nefarious poop crimes. It works like this: First, I choose a suspect. Let's use Bucky for this example. His whereabouts cannot be confirmed for the time in question. The others all have alibis.

Next, I must determine the location of the evidence BEFORE I step in it, or else I lose. In case that wasn't obvious. Does the offender have a go-to crime scene? Do I recall hearing anything—creaking floorboards or telltale clicking paw-falls—that would indicate where the dark deposit was made? Today, I'm thinking the parlor. (I really do have a parlor. Because evidently it's 1847.)

Lastly, I narrow down the weaponry. Does the suspect have a signature expulsion? Did he or she ingest something suspicious? Hmm, today I'm gonna say ... diarrhea. (On days when I'm feeling really smart, I will add a subcategory to the chosen vehicle, like "foamy" or "Jesus Christ, is that my hot-pink earbud?" but this is risky. Not intended for rookies.)

So, class, today's sleuthing results in ... say it with me: Bucky in the Parlor with Foamy Diarrhea. *moonwalks to cabinet housing impressive cleaning product supply*

Other possible combinations include Meatball in the Hallway with a Hairball, Karma in the Laundry Room with Half-Eaten-Mouse Vomit (and <u>FUCK ME</u> if that fluffy bitch didn't steal my last Valium), Hashbrown in the Bedroom with Bat Barf, Lizzie Borden on the Bed with the Biggest Shit I've Ever Seen in My Entire Life (Seriously, I could transcribe *Anna Karenina* on that shit. But that would be gross.), Stevie Nicks in the Kitchen with Pee (At least I think it's pee. Could be bile. Will have to smell to confirm.). You get the picture.

The great thing is that anyone can play! Pets, children, husbands—you can now make ALL your life's messes just a little more fun. And not to toot my own horn (*toot-toot!*), but if I'm not mistaken, it would appear that I have just invented the only game in the whole history of time where, literally, nobody wins.

And that? Is awesome.

10 / my top 10 totally rational fears

1. Vomit: In real life, my fear of vomit is so well-documented that there is barely need to mention it. My friends know, my family knows, the UPS guy knows, and my therapist definitely knows. However, for those who are not yet aware—I don't *do* vomit. I don't want to see it, I don't want to hear about it, I don't want to talk about it, I don't want to know about it. I don't want to hear it happening and I certainly don't want to smell it.

I promise you, I will run screaming, even if the vomit only appears on a TV or movie screen.

I will not hold your hair back while you do it. I will not clean it up. I will not even talk to you on the phone if you have a vomit-bug, because I will obviously catch it.

It is, I am certain, my maniacal aversion to upchuck that has prevented me from becoming a dreadful, slobbering drunk or peyote-smoking lunatic—such revelry results all too often in the blowing of chunks. I have barfed exactly twice since the age of ten—both times from tuna fish—and have no plans to do it again, ever. I think we're done here.

2. Self-Checkout Lanes: Who *isn't* afraid of these atrocious grocery-store Dementors? They lure you in with the promise of a quick, small-talk-free escape and total freedom to purchase your embarrassing personal products in perfect anonymity—away from the prying eyes of unctuous checkout harpies (who totally think you're a slut) and pimply teen clerks (who totally HOPE you're a slut)—just to hurl you headlong under the Shame Train that only rattles by when the goddamn laser-thingy fails to scan your Yeast-B-Gone, requiring clamorous assistance from the very same horny teens and checkout harpies you wanted so to avoid. You win, fuckers.

3. Umbrellas: It's the terrible little teeth and ruthless pinching places. Opening them is fine—pleasant, even. Satisfying. Makes you feel like you've accomplished something. *Click!* But closing? It's a goddamn death trap. Hence my lusty embrace of foul weather—hair, suede, and sequins be damned. I'd rather be sodden and woebegone than dry and bleeding out.[1]

4. Squiggly Text Tests: You know those twisty, illegible letters on the computer that you are supposed to somehow decipher and retype into a tiny box to prove ... what? That you are a wizard with magical eyesight, obviously. It's supposed to be some sort of clever trick to derail the robot overlords (I mean, what a time to be alive!) who are evidently poised to commandeer your friend's mommy blog, but instead triggers you into a soul-crushing shame spiral.

Debilitating typing terror?

1. Please see All-You-Can-Eat Crab Legs Buffet for the obvious exception. If you aren't bleeding, you're doing it wrong.

Check.

Inevitable failure to reproduce said nonsense letters?

Check.

Self-loathing tailspin?

Check.

Enjoy your revenge, you geek bastards.

5. Pull-Down Ladders: High atop my list of Personal Horrors and/or Universal Abominations sit these agents of certain and excruciating demise.

I understand that lots of people keep things in their attics that they might like to access at some point. But I do NOT understand what the hell you've got up there that it's worth dying to get it down.

Rigged precisely to *plummet violently down from directly above your head,* there is simply no escaping decapitation if you choose to take this death-bait. And if by some miracle you survive the pulling-down portion of the horror show, just try pushing it back up again. Let's just say the Reaper doesn't miss twice.

If you're OK with that, knock yourself out. Me? I'm just gonna clear some space in the garage.

6. Steely Dan: I have no explanation. All I have is this creeping —and very real—dread in my soul every time I hear the awful strains of Doom's Own Minstrels drifting though the ether. I have no recollection of being tortured or bullied or water-boarded with Steely Dan playing in the background. As far as I know, I was not kiddie-diddled by a Steely Dan superfan or made to listen to it while someone ate my kitten. I truly cannot understand it.

"Hey Nineteen" in particular inspires in me a terror akin to bobbing alone in shark-infested seas with a bloody stump where my foot used to be. A million miles from shore, in the black of night, and no one's coming for me. Actually, now that I spell it out, that sounds like a much better way to go than dying of Steely Dan.

7. Albuquerque: Not the place—before you get all indignant and "New Mexicans are people, too!" on me. Trying to spell it is what scares me. My fear mounts exponentially with every failed attempt to write it properly, and inevitably I just end up putting something like "Abba-Kacky" so it appears as though I am kicky and convivial. I am neither. I just hate that shit-sucking word—with the fire of a thousand suns, I hate it. "Eighth" is no picnic either, if I'm being honest.

8. Remote Controls: Since when does everyone have, like, seven remotes for one goddamned screen? And how does ANYONE figure out which goes to what gadget, and which one is for what streaming service and what combination of buttons and handhelds will magically find me my goddamned *Letterkenny*? And what about when you totally cock it up and everything goes black or staticky and you have no idea what you did so you have no idea how to undo it and the noise from the static is making you feel like you need to hide, or kill someone, and all you can do is cry because at this point you don't even know how to turn it off? Then what? Huh?![2]

---

2. This particular terror pretty much applies to all technology. And anything with wires. Or buttons. And what the fuck is a dongle? Actually, don't tell me. Whatever it is, I'm certain that I'm not prepared to handle it.

9. Skin Suits and the People Who Make Them: I'm quite sure I have my mother to thank for this one. "Pretty young thing gets turned into skin suit by masher" was one of her signature scare scenarios. As a result, I assume everyone I meet is sizing me up (literally) to determine what sort of outfit they could make out of me. I happen to think I'd be a fantastic poodle skirt.

Because skin-sewing is never far from my mind, when I hear the incessant, rhythmic squeaking of the swings from the playground next door I do not assume that neighborhood children are out for a joyful morning romp. I naturally ascertain that I have awakened to the Zombie End Times, and my entire town has been made into a giant flesh tuxedo by axe-wielding survivalists and that perhaps my supple hide is simply being saved for a jazzy ascot. Is that weird?

10. Too-Long Naps: Taking a nap is scary enough, obviously—I'm not doing work! I'm a delinquent! Why am I so tired? Am I dying? Oh my god, I'm totally dying—but when it lasts longer than intended, it's downright terrifying—especially if you wake up and it's turned dark outside. Holy crap! It's nighttime—did I sleep through my whole life? Did I just Rip Van Winkle that shit? Did I miss DINNER? Do I have to go to bed again soon? What day is it? Fuck, I am in soooo much trouble. *Please do not tell my mother.*

11 / red solo cup, my lord and savior

Guyarrhea: *The sudden-onset, DEFCON-one urgency to evacuate one's bowels at the appearance—or mere thought, in extreme cases—of one's crush. This condition is incurable.*

As a teen and young adult, my very best memories were made in the lush, quiet forests of Pennsylvania's Pocono Mountains. I'd been going there with my family every summer since I was a baby, as had both of my parents. The hotel where we stayed as a family was stately and exclusive, steeped in the old-world elegance and upper-crust pageantry that my parents dearly hoped would eventually take hold in my inelegant, heathen-adjacent soul. (Spoiler alert: It did not.)

We're talking consommé (it's meat Jell-O and don't let anyone tell you otherwise), finger bowls, dress codes in the dining room, golf games and tennis lessons, and some unholy contrivance called the Grand March, wherein good little children performed like circus animals every Saturday night, parading our way through stations in the ballroom while old fucks in seersucker looked on and assessed our curtsying skills. There was literally not one thing I hated more as a child. I tried EVERYTHING to get out of it: feigning illness, crying, begging, even hiding atop the ridiculously high diving board one year in an attempt to evade capture (I really fucked my seven-year-old self there, because the only way off was to death-plunge four stories down into the freezing lake). It never worked. So I marched. I curtsied. And I cursed my parents to the seventh fucking circle of hell, resolving to never stop making them pay for this.

So imagine my uncontainable delight when, a few years later, I discovered that there was a neighboring resort just up the road. WITH BOYS. And beer. And parent-free parties and campouts and pot and waterfalls and, um, BOYS. There was a veritable fucking *Dirty Dancing* situation happening a mere croquet-mallet's-throw away, and I knew that I, and Satan, had finally won. I even obtained my mother's permission—nay, blessing!—to go hang out with my new friends, who I had convinced her were finger-bowl-dipping mofos with the kind of expensive pedigrees she'd always longed for me to long for. And in truth, they were those things: every bit as privileged and entitled as I was, just with a whole lot less supervision.

Eventually, I defected completely and started spending whole summers there, staying with the family of two brothers I'd befriended. *Fuckin' A*, we had fun. We were just rich kids pretending to be hippies, stealing golf carts, playing spin-the-bottle, sleeping under the stars, and building friendships closer and more bonded than any others I'd ever had. It was the only place I wanted to be, and they were the only friends I wanted to see. Summer's end was always heart-wrenching, signaling a return to the repression and depression of my other life. Year after year, the only thing that kept me going was the knowledge that, on December 31, we'd reunite in those mountains for a bomb-ass kegger that would bridge the lonely gap between summers.

The summer before my freshman year in college, I suffered

a debilitating and unrequited crush on an older boy that gloomily followed me all the way back to school. The crush. Not the boy. I was a wreck, completely uninterested in the preppy assholes that populated the campus and simply counting the days until New Year's.

Look, I have always been boy crazy—I mean, ya girl wrote literal love letters to John Denver at age five (and he wrote me back TWICE!)—though utterly inept at flirting and absolutely all talk, no action. I had the filthiest mind of anyone I knew, but to my great dismay, my body was mostly untouched. I fumbled every single opportunity to engage with cute boys: I'd either trip, snort, get hives, say idiotic things, freeze in horror, or, most often, get slammed with a catastrophic gastrointestinal emergency that required immediate evacuation from the scene. The severity of the guyarhhea attack was, obviously, in direct proportion to how cute the boy was and/or how much I liked him. I was a hot, hot pants-mess.

But this time, I had four months to prepare my game and win my crush. I knew I had to get this shit under control, literally, and as New Year's approached, I hatched a plan: I simply wouldn't eat for a few days and, to be absolutely safe, I'd pre-take Imodium AND Pepto-Bismol before the party. I'd create such a leaden shutdown of my bowels that John Denver himself couldn't get them rumbling.

The night arrived, finally, and, back in our beloved mountains after months away, we prepared to fucking party. Snow crunched beneath our feet as we made our way toward the fragrant smoke curling out of the lone chimney in those beautiful woods, and the night felt perfect. We were all appropriately festive and glittered up for the occasion, but I had taken special care to look AMAZING. This was the eighties, mind you. That meant enormous hair (with requisite ear tunnels, achieved through the violent wielding of a painfully bristled round brush and half a can of Aqua Net per tunnel), aggressive shoulder padding, clownishly bright architectural makeup, and stirrup pants. Of course, stirrup pants. I was not fucking around.

Some idiot back at college had once told me that I had beautiful clavicles (really dude?? OK), so naturally I made sure that those things were moisturized, perfumed, highlighted, and fully, freezingly exposed. (Clearly, I didn't get many compliments.)

I was ready. Game-fucking-ON. I was going to talk to him, bat my damn eyelashes, *possibly* even make out with him, and I was NOT going to shit my pants. *THIS IS WHAT YOU'VE BEEN TRAINING FOR, MARIE. You got this.*

To my immense surprise, his face lit up when he saw me (I told you, I looked amazing) and he came right over to greet me with a hug, followed by a hungry leer at my exposed (and apparently magical?) clavicles. He raised his eyebrows and purred, "Wow, you look good."

That was all it took. Within seconds, I felt it. Guyarrhea. Nooooooo.

My stomach lurched and my whole body flushed with cold sweat. I took the deep, calming breaths I'd been practicing and reminded myself that I was a strong, capable woman and that I'd taken the necessary precautions to prevent a rectal Armageddon, but it was futile. It was happening. Oh God.

COME ON, MARIE. WE TALKED ABOUT THIS.

Nope. The umami tsunami was absolutely on its way, barreling toward freedom.

I calmly pretended to get something in my eye, excused myself from that sexy motherfucker, and began making my way to the single bathroom in the tiny cabin that currently housed about thirty heavy-drinking revelers. There was, predictably, a huge line. (Ratios: aka why I hate math.)

I wasn't gonna make it.

I clenched and shuffled and death-gripped my red Solo cup and prayed to all the gods I knew to please, please get me out of this.

I'll do better, I swear. I'll be nicer to my mom. I'll wear the fucking penny loafers. I'll do annnyyything, pleeeasssee, I begggg youuuuuuu.

I must have made it, because the next thing I remember is getting into the tiny bathroom and locking the door behind me. I'd barely gotten my clothes and underwear out of the line of fire before I unleashed hell upon the poor porcelain bowl and, I suspect, several other nearby surfaces. All the months of waiting, wishing, pining over a beautiful boy, and dreaming of a New Year's kiss had finally climaxed in a display of gastric devastation the likes of which no one could have prepared for.

But then it was over. Sweet, sweet relief. Now I could breathe. I was mortified, but would obviously claim that any lingering smell had already been there when I went in. I worked out what I'd say and whom I'd finger as the culprit for the stench, and contentedly went to flush the toilet.

Nothing.

Please, God. No.

I tried again. And again. Nope.

CODE BROWN. I REPEAT, CODE BROWN.

Again, and nothing. Nothing but silence (and roughly sixteen pounds of liquid horror) in the bowl. My terror was growing by the second, and at this point I was pretty sure that I'd be momentarily adding barf to the unholy chowder below. The line was growing outside the door, and impatient drunks threatened to breach the perimeter between them and this brown carnage. Tears threatened to ruin my meticulously applied makeup and sully my perfect clavicles.

There was simply no way out of this. I'd have to confess.

Unless ... the window. *YES.*

Hail the Old Gods! Bless this tiny aperture and its old-timey crank handle. I'd climb out into the freezing night and simply disappear. Never to be seen again. No coat, no shoes, no contest. If my choices were (1) owning up to this ghastly ass massacre, or (2) *death*? I chose death, obviously. I refused to surrender my dignity to a lifetime as the girl whose asshole single-holedly destroyed a century of perfectly good plumbing. No way.

As I sat perched, mid-hoist, with my butt out the window preparing to flop backward into the snowbank beneath like a scuba diving turd-terrorist, I saw it:

Red. Plastic. Perfect.

My Solo cup. My salvation.

I swore I heard the angels sing and baby Jesus himself weep (I mean, he probably did, though, actually. Just not for the reasons I thought.) as I jumped down from the windowsill, triumphantly raised my Solo cup in a toast to my own brilliance, and commenced scooping the accursed consommé out of the toilet and into the snowdrift outside. I was saved. I would not die this night.

Catastrophe averted, I closed the window, washed my hands, and emerged as cool as a poopsicle from the small bathroom where my life had briefly flashed before my eyes as I willingly readied to trade it for the last remaining shred of my dignity.

I issued a dismissive heads-up about the flusher being wonky to the horde of drunks waiting in line outside the bathroom and headed back to the party, head high and clavicles gleaming. I needed a stiff fucking drink and, yes, a fresh cup.

I often think of this story and wonder what I'd do now, thirty-six years later, if the same thing happened again. Am I even still capable, after all this time and so much soul-death, of the kind of heartbreakingly hopeful excitement that would cause my bowels to instantly explode at the sight of a cute guy? Probably not. Would I be so mortified by the thought of clogging a friend's toilet that I would climb out a window and risk freezing to death in a mountain forest (or entering Witness Protection) rather than fess the fuck up? Nah. Do I still believe that my value hinges upon the relative contents—or lack thereof—of the bowl beneath my butt? I absolutely do not.

Will I ever again enter a strange bathroom without a red Solo cup in hand?

FUCK. NO.

12 / bite me. no, seriously

As I write this, glorious, jewel-toned leaves rustle and fall outside my window. The last of my tomatoes sit poignantly on the vine among the withered and brown remains of my once-abundant summer garden. The air is crisp and fragrant with wood smoke, and basic bitches everywhere are bulk-buying pumpkin-spice everything—lattes, muffins, tampons—like they're going out of style. Which, evidently, they are not. Ever.

You know what that means?

It's Vampire Season, y'all.

Well, it's always Vampire Season if you're me, but at this time of year, the rest of the world seems to not only tolerate my bizarre fixation, but to share it. This is fantastic news, because honestly? It's exhausting trying to nourish a non-seasonal craving. Ever tried to find a candy cane in July, when its bracing, minty vigor would make a most refreshing treat? Or a ripe, juicy peach in December? Exactly.

But still, this shit just doesn't make sense. It would obviously be much easier to ~~seduce~~ terminate a ~~sexy-as-hell~~ psychotic immortal murderer using my luscious carotid cleavage as bait during the warmer months, but this is not the way of things.

I have a friend with the titanium nutsack to rock a full-on cape year-round, for virtually any reason at all, and without the slightest concern for societal or seasonal raised eyebrows. He's like, "Yes, I am wearing a cape. And?"

And he's not even a vampire. I envy his bravado. And his collection of fine opera-wear.

As it stands, this is the only time of year when I can voice some of my more pressing concerns about the undead without people thinking I'm any weirder than they usually think I am. Which is pretty fucking weird, but that's beside the point. The media have, frankly, confounded me to the point where I don't even really know the proper way to dispatch a vampire anymore. There are too many choices, too many discrepancies, too many liberties being taken in the modern lore. It's irresponsible, honestly. I mean, isn't this *kind of* a matter of life and death? I would simply like a straight answer on a few things.

Used to be, a wooden stake through the heart—and ONLY a wooden stake through the heart—would do the trick. And while this method of termination is still considered a fail-safe classic, it seems it's not our only choice anymore. And let's face it—who really ever *has* a pointy wooden stake on hand unless you live in Sunnydale or Transylvania (or Washington, DC)? Nobody, that's who.

So let's break this down. There are a few TV and movie franchises that really fly in the face of everything we know about vampires (and have known for hundreds of years), and they need to answer for a few things. Who, pray tell, do they think they are? And more importantly, who do they think WE are? Uninformed blockheads? Dullards? Dolts?

First up, let's check in with the *Vampire Diaries* and Mystic Falls' own sexy Salvatore brothers, the undead offenders in question. Damon is snarky, hilarious, and uber-hot and makes the hands-down best crazy eyes I have ever seen, ever. Brother Stephan is broody, dark, romantic, and deep, which totally doesn't matter because all you can do is stare at his oft-exposed abs. Stephan WILL give you pants-feelings. Unless you are already dead, and then it gets slightly more complicated. Actually, not really—you'll just have slightly more complicated pants-feelings.

Stephan's insider-vamp-nickname is the Ripper, due to his savage feeding style and fondness for leaving brutal carnage behind after a kill. And you're like, "Yeah, I'm totally OK with that—as long as he takes his shirt off at some point."

These teen vamps drink a lot of alcohol (in addition to blood)—from very fancy crystal decanters. I like to think it's bourbon, because that's totally what I would drink if I were a sexy, misunderstood vampire just trying to fit in. They also eat. Like, food.

This is in direct violation of every rule we've ever been taught about the undead. EVERYONE KNOWS VAMPIRES DO NOT EAT. GOD!

And this is where I get pissy. Because you can also kill these fuckers with wooden bullets and some botanical concoction called *vervain.* Is vervain even a thing? (My spellcheck suggests not.) And if it is, may I please have some so that I can kill some goddamn vampires? Or at least bang them?

Sunlight is another element that enrages me—in general, certainly, but more specifically, in nouveau vamp contexts. The ever-growing vampire population of Mystic Falls can freely walk in daylight as long as they are wearing a magic ring made for them by the town witch. (Yep. Mystic Falls has witches. Werewolves, too. And somehow I still do not live there.) Sans ring, things get ugly and the usual sizzling flesh and festering face-melt ensues. At least some things are sacred.

Then there are the *Twilight* trilogy's Cullen vampires of

Forks, WA, who as we all know, sparkle when direct sunlight is applied. ***They ... sparkle.*** I ... can't ... let's just move on.

John Mitchell, the second-hottest-vampire-ever and his nasty undead colleagues on *Being Human* (UK version, obvs) don't seem to even address the sunlight issue at all, which is really inconsiderate, honestly. Because there might be *someone* out there who is earnestly trying to understand, and who feels confused by this glaring omission and cannot really even concentrate on the awesome vampires because they should NOT BE WALKING AROUND OUTSIDE.

deep breath

regroup

Anyway, I'm totally just pretending to want to know how to kill vampires, because that's what a *normal* person should do when faced with a ravenous immortal lunatic who is trying to exsanguinate her. What I'd really like to do is let them eat me, in exchange for immortality. Yes, there is something quite wrong with me. But clearly, I am not the only sicko out there. Women go bananas for this shit.

The *Twilight* vampires have probably saved more marriages than Oprah just by virtue of their waxen bangability. (Sorry, friends—unless you ARE one of the Cullen Crew of Forks, WA, your partner is probably not thinking about you when you're bumpin' fuzz. Just FYI.) Edward is, of course, everyone's undead It Boy, until the moment in Part 2 when he removes his shirt and exposes what can only politely be called a Nipular Incongruity. I've devoted my life to trying to unsee that. It's not going well.

TV's Angel? Total babe. Michael from the movie *Lost Boys* is so sexy that his eighties 'do actually still looks good on him. Vampire Brad Pitt is just Brad Pitt with, like, exponentially cracked-out hotness. Vampire Tom Cruise is ... a pale, frilly fancy-man who ... yeah. Never mind. Still better than regular Tom Cruise, I suppose.

Finally, with no offense to all of the undead eye candy aforementioned, ALL other vampires are merely immortal buffoons next to the inimitable Gary Oldman, whose Dracula will always be my top pick for escort to the Prom of Eternal Damnation.

His portrayal of the Count is flawless, heartbreaking, super-sexy, and terrifying all at once—and does not leave me wondering how I would kill him, at ALL, because I am totally trying to figure out a way to get him to kill ME so I can be his Dark Lady Succubus forever. And ever. And ever. Don't lie. You do it, too.

Why, though? Why are homicidal dead dudes so appealing to women (and men with exquisite taste in capery)? What does it say about our level of relative safety and control that all we want to do is abandon everything we hold dear and get ourselves murdered by some bloodthirsty fiends?

Is it really about them?

Or is it about us? And all of the things that women have to tend to, care for, worry about, organize, facilitate, and perfect for the living humans in our world? I mean, you never see lady vampires have to get a goddamn Pap smear and then go home and clean up dog shit, help their vamp kids with math homework, and cook dinner for their dad-bodied, emotionally unavailable vamp husbands. They are far too busy lurking in shadows, serving haute-goth lewks while they prepare to lure their next meal to its untimely demise. There is velvet involved. Always.

Maybe eternal damnation just sounds heavenly in its absolute self-indulgence. You eat when you want and who you want. You sleep all day. You are young forever. And you used a beautiful boy to get there. Delicious and diabolical.

Perhaps immortality is simply liberation. With fangs.

But probably it's just because they're hot. Who are we kidding?

There is, I believe, only one fitting way to end this chapter—and that's with the wise, immortal words of *The Lost Boys*' Sam Emerson: "You're a vampire, Michael. My own brother, a goddamn shit-suckin' vampire. You wait till Mom finds out, buddy."

Because she'll totally want to sleep with you.

13 / a sexter's guide to the galaxy (generally, avoid uranus)

Guys. Sexting? Is awesome. I am a HUGE fan of sexting.

> *Disclaimer: If you are a teenaged girl, please do not send naked pictures of yourself to your boyfriend. Teen boys are helpless little shits, especially when it comes to boobies. It's not their fault. They are biologically obligated to show their friends, and YOUR NAKED PICTURE WILL END UP ON THE INTERNET FOREVER. Just don't do it.*

Anyway, I, a fully formed and mostly functioning adult, love sexting. And I don't mind telling you, I'm pretty goddamn good at it. It's so easy with the right playmate. I mean, low-stakes, low-effort, no-cost fun? That I can have on my own couch? Yes, please.

I mean, the only thing that needs to be looking hot or smelling fresh for me to KILL IT sexting is my enviably filthy lexicon, which is, I humbly submit, top-tier. I can be sending the lewdest, *Penthouse Forum*-iest content to my cellularly intended whilst wearing flannel pajamas, Coke-bottle glasses, TMJ mouthguard, and tube socks, with two cats on my head and a nosebleed. He doesn't need to know that instead of writhing around in a vat of strippers, cherries, and coconut oil as advertised, I'm watching *Saved by the Bell* and eating Bugles (Witch Fingers!).

Here's why I'm so good—it's because I actually mean it. If given the chance and the miracle of good timing, huge lady-balls, and a lawless society, I would be doing exactly what I say I'd be doing. To exactly whom I say I'd be doing it.

I don't sext with anyone I wouldn't actually have all the real sex with, given the above conditions. And it hurts no one (unless one or both of you is in another relationship, which is a whole other can of sex worms that I don't recommend you open).

It's fun. It's secret. It's clean.

I don't *do* casual sex. Never have. It's far too dangerous and it's just ... well ... awkward. The ONE time I decided I'd really go wild and have totally safe, protected sex with someone who wasn't my boyfriend or husband, the condom came off and got STUCK IN MY VAGINA FOR 24 HOURS (the thing's like a steel trap, what can I tell you?) and I spent the entire next day—as per instructions procured on the internet—shooting warm water up there with a turkey baster and fisting myself in an effort to retrieve the lost condom without a visit to the ER. Like, there's even an insurance code for that.

I made the grave mistake of sharing this—um, mishap?—with a close male friend, who still refers to me as Old Southpaw and swears he'll never come for Thanksgiving.

You see? Sexting can be a very good option for someone like me, or you! Generally, it's a lot cleaner, and not just biohazard-wise. It's emotionally cleaner as well. It could be someone you haven't seen in years or someone whose path will never cross yours in real life, making it unlikely your snaps will land in, say, your brother's group chat. There's nothing to lose, really. It's the whole point.

You can see them however you want to see them, or however their Instagram wants you to see them—and vice versa. There's no backne or halitosis or sauerkraut BO on his end to contend with, and frankly, you don't have to wax or aerate or hide your wobbly bits in order to get handily rogered via sext.

You don't have to worry about accidentally farting in the middle of it, or accidentally farting in your sleep afterward, or accidentally farting in the morning when you pee in his bathroom because you've held in the fart all fucking night long and it just slips out because it won't freaking wait any longer and *fuuuuck, please tell me he did not just hear that* (he totally did).

Sexting is virtually worry free in the Fart Department. Fart away! He'll never know.

And all the while YOU know it's all an illusion. And your heart is as safe as your lady business.

But what happens when, at like 1:30 in the afternoon on a Tuesday, you find yourself wondering what kind of sandwich he might get for lunch that day. Or how many brothers and sisters he has, or what makes him laugh—really laugh, from the belly, not just LOL, as evidenced by the cry/laughing emoji indicating hilarity.

What happens when you realize that you almost just actually water-shat your pants when he texted unexpectedly because you have managed to work yourself and your stomach up into such school-girly knots over him that your bowels are no longer your own?

What happens when you find yourself reasoning that the ridiculous age difference between you or the geographical impossibilities of your arrangement or the fact that you have good reason to suspect *he might be a Republican* are nothing but mild nuisances?

What happens when you realize—to your abject horror—

that you actually LIKE him? For fuckssake, then what?! That was not part of the plan.

How would that GO, anyway, for argument's sake? I mean, how would one even begin to move the conversation in that direction? "Baby, I will make you a nutritionally sound breakfast SO hard ..." or "You can watch while I slowwwwly pull up to the curb, take off my seatbelt, and pick up your mother for her podiatrist appointment. Mmmm ..." Or "I am sooooo hot right now, babe. I think it's the menopause."

Yeah, it's awkward.

Not to mention the fact that the only way to find out if your accursed "feelings" are mutual is to risk (a) cocking up a perfectly thermonuclear tickle party in your pants, and (b) getting really hurt and terribly embarrassed—which defies the Ultimate and Universal Law of Sexting: ***It's Just Sext, You Idiot***.

Plus, HE OBVIOUSLY SMELLS LIKE SAUERKRAUT. Never forget that. He has to.

The problem is, of course, that once you feel something, you can't really just *unfeel* it. You've crossed a line, and the course goes in one direction all the way to the end of the story. The options are few: Carry on as is and pretend you don't care while you water-shit your pants every time you hear from him, or fess the fuck up. And honestly? For most of us, death by Krazy Glue sounds better than either of those.

So I ask you: Why is it so much easier to say *Baby, I'm gonna ___ your ___ until you ___ and then I'm gonna ___ while ___ my* ___ than it is to say *Hey, I kinda like you. For real.* ???

Finally, there is the choice just to stop. Disappear into the ether, never to be sexted from again. And that's the worst one of all. But it's the one most of us will choose, if the alternative is exposing ourselves to potential heartbreak or, even more terrifying, the possibility of the universe hatching an actual relationship.

So sext away, friends. Sext away. Strengthen those thumbs and get good at taking naked selfies. But make no mistake: However disengaged you intend to remain, however detached you assume your tech-only affair will keep you, your heart is not, in fact, as safe as your lady business. Take it from this intrepid sexter, who has, on at least one unfortunate occasion, found herself deep in a pickle for her cause, and not the other way around.

14 / my brother, beelzebub

As I'm quite sure you've gathered by now, life with my mother has always been high drama. Nowhere was this more apparent than in her many health challenges. No diagnosis or doctor's axiom was simply "You have this thing. Take that thing and you'll be fine." She was pretty much a Walking Murphy's Law (Medical Edition).

What could go wrong *would* go wrong, and in spectacular fashion; then she'd—with her pioneering spirit—invent a slew of new things to go wrong.

What I understand now is that her debilitating anxiety and depression made it almost impossible for her to heal her physical body. Her brain was too busy manufacturing the chaos that took its tangible toll on her health (in addition to taking its toll on the rest of us).

One of those things turned out to be her heart—a leaky valve that required a replacement. My parents had divorced by this time—thank the gods—so it was on me and my brothers to help her through it. For me, that meant packing up my car with my heinous husband and his equally heinous offspring and leaving Utah's glorious cool summer to die from heat exhaustion in New Jersey for the duration of her recovery. The only reason they came with me was because he didn't have a job and would have no way to support himself and his kid without me there to foot the bills. So it was. Dogs, cats, leeches, and me. Crammed in a car headed for what we all knew would be a disaster on every front.

The night before her procedure was to take place, she checked into Columbia Presbyterian Hospital in NYC for pre-op tests, only to be told that the doctors could not do the operation. The arteries around her heart were dangerously calcified, and if even one tiny fragment of that eggshell coating was dislodged during the procedure (and there was a high likelihood that it would be), she would stroke out and die. Mom was an insurance nightmare, and there was no one there who felt safe performing the replacement. Without the surgery, she would die anyway, just less expediently. Dead if you do and dead if you don't. The surgical team, though, wouldn't budge.

In fact, we were told, there was only one surgeon in the country that could do it. And whether he *would* do it remained to be seen. That surgeon was Dr. Craig Smith, the man who had gained notoriety for successfully performing the same procedure on Bill Clinton some years before. No one knew where he was or if he was available, but they assured us that they would try.

They did find him and he did agree to operate on my mother. As I recall there was great and urgent fanfare around his arrival—a helicopter on the hospital roof, lots of bustling nurses barking medical code—as my brothers and I sat tensely in the waiting area, helpless to do anything but watch it unfold. We were hopeful, but urged by the staff to not be *too* hopeful. This was still insanely dangerous.

But he did it. After something like eight hours, during which we told each other that every hour that went by with no word was good news, Dr. Smith emerged to say that the procedure was done and that Mom had survived. We crumpled into each other with relief and elation. We loved her (and each other) so much in that moment, it seemed that the worst was behind us and we could handle whatever else was to come with great fucking aplomb.

LOL.

Of course, recovery was hell. They had bone-sawed through her breastbone, for fuckssake. It would be awful for anyone. But my mother was not anyone.

She was feral.

The recovery wing reverberated with her unceasing shrieks and wails; from ghostly howls to ear-splitting screams, she called out for her long-dead father and cursed the archfiends who had saved her life. She repeatedly and unironically demanded to see Dr. Kevorkian (also, by that time, quite dead). I shit you not. From every corner of the floor, at every time of day, her screams echoed.

The projected two weeks in the hospital became eight, of course. My brothers and I turned up dutifully each day to offer (unsuccessfully) some comfort to her, to the nursing staff, to each other. It all backfired. The atrocious behavior was unspeakably painful: the culmination of so many years of shame and embarrassment, added to our shared failure to stop or even de-escalate it. We turned on each other, frequently, but were quick to reconcile, knowing we had no other choice. Unite or die.

Eventually, the staff began to slip her some Xanax along with her many other medications, and it brought quick but temporary relief to all of us. This was a frequent trick employed by her medical caretakers over the years: adding a simple antidepressant or antianxiety med to her regimen after this infection or that procedure. “This will help you heal faster,” they told her.

And so it did—until eventually she figured out that she was taking mental health drugs and would fly into a fury of blame and indignation. It never lasted long, but those were good days.

As those days turned to weeks turned to months, she became more manageable despite having every possible complication arise. She was able to have brief conversations to ask how her dogs or horses or finches were doing. She still had monstrous moments, but as her pain and fear abated, so did some of the more beastly behavior.

The drains still protruded out of her back like sterile tentacles, and she sported other barbaric contraptions meant to keep her from accumulating fluid in her lungs or rebreaking her cracked bones. She would have still much preferred to die, as she reminded us daily.

One day, the floor was abuzz with the arrival of a celebrity doctor and, assuming it was Dr. Death himself, my mother was *sure* her ship had finally come in.

I was in high favor that day (I think I'd smuggled in some frothy treat from Starbucks for her), but my oldest brother Billy was FUCKED.[1] He had encouraged her, gently and kindly, to do her breathing exercises, which she loathed. Rather than rage at him, she icily asked me for her Transgression Journal instead, so she could document this latest infraction. (She had one for each of us and our respective spouses, and, I presume, every doctor, friend, employee, pet, and post office clerk who had the gall to cross her in any way. Stacks of them. How in the fresh-fuck else was she supposed to keep track of our every offense? HUH?)

1. Archie was always in good standing. He'd had the good sense to peace out of NJ decades earlier and hardly ever saw her, so he was kind and patient with her when he did. Unlike me and Billy.

Aaaaaaanyway, when Dr. Infomercial came in the room to spread his celebrity cheese, my mother disappointedly exclaimed, "YOU'RE not Dr. Kevorkian! Who will administer my lethal injection?"

"No, ma'am," he chuckled, cheesily. "I'm Dr. X." (I refuse to speak his name after the last election cycle.)

"Oh, how lovely to meet you, Doctor. Two of my children are here today. Might I introduce you to my astonishingly beautiful, smart, and talented daughter, Marie"—she beamed —"and my son ..." Here, her face contorted theatrically and her lips curled into a grotesque snarl as she bellowed in a three-octaves-deeper, guttural roar, "BEELZEBUB!"

"Pleasure to meet you both," he tittered nervously, and *fucked the fuck right off* out of that room faster than he could later pretend to be a Pennsylvania resident. I tried to hold in my laughter as Billy silently looked over at me. Resigned, amused, amazed. Heartbroken.

I felt for him in that moment, but let's face it, I was beautiful and perfect that day and I intended to milk that shit hard. Plus, I now had that Biblical comic gold in my pocket forever and I was not going to waste it. I'm not a fucking psychopath.

Eventually, Mom got out of the hospital and returned home to continue her rehabilitation with a whole new unsuspecting team of caretakers to torment. She remembered virtually nothing of her time at Columbia Pres. Or so she claimed. It seemed the trauma of those two months was ours alone.

Archie returned to his quieter life in FL. I went back to Utah with my own two demons in tow, altered once again by the breadth of our family's peripheral damage. Billy remained, ever faithful to my mother and her care. The debt we owe him is unpayable.

It is years later now. The pain of that long ordeal has receded somewhat, and our own hearts have mostly healed from the unholy memories of that hospital floor (I assumed they smudged the shit out of it after our mom checked out). Still, every now and then, I have no choice but to remind Billy of the day I was perfect.

"Yo, B'zubs, whuddup! Make any blood sacrifices today?"

"What time will you be summoning your demon army? I'll make dinner."

"Did you know that your name in Hebrew translates to 'Lord of Dung'?"

I am, dear reader, a dick. I know this. I can take things too far. I can use my words unwisely. I can be crass, and unfeeling, and hurtful, and unforgiving.

But *Jesus*. At least I'm not a goddamned baby-eating dung lord.

Like my brother.

15 / swimsuit issues

HEY, REMEMBER THAT time a decade or so ago when *Sports Illustrated* dared to put an allegedly "plus-sized" model (heavy emphasis on the air quotes) in the pages of their swimsuit issue? Yeah, that was fun.

In case you were visiting Amish Country at the time, or blissfully stranded in some Amazonian, No Boys Allowed rainforest, or—GOD FORBID!—have better things to do than worry about how much other people weigh, the ogress in question was Robyn Lawley, a gorgeous, leggy, size-12 Australian supermodel who made news and raised many eyebrows for being the first "plus-sized" woman to be featured in the pages of *Sports Illustrated*'s iconic Swimsuit Issue. Jesus Fucking Christ. I don't even know where to start.

Because when I say "raised eyebrows," I mean "incited a million rage-filled rants by hairy Neanderthals" who took to the internet to bemoan the loss of their beloved *Sports Illustrated* to Eyeball-Charring Fat People. Said Neanderthals seized the ether to hereby declare the End of Civilization, citing the "everybody gets a trophy" culture as the limp-wristed, liberal propagandist responsible for ushering in the age where, if anybody is allowed to win, everybody surely loses.

A friend(!) of mine articulated his disappointment on Facebook by analogizing the "Fat Lady Issue" to a car magazine misleading potential readers by promising Ferraris and Lamborghinis and delivering, instead, a spread featuring a taupe Ford Taurus. Another friend, more earnest in his desire for open dialogue, said, "But she admitted she's a size 12. It's not like anyone's falsely accusing her."

That's right, SHE ADMITTED IT. Oh my god. Next thing you know she's going to "admit" to goat sex or coprophagia. Or *eating*.

Standards are extinct, they said. It's not our job to make chubby girls feel good about themselves, they said. They're promoting obesity, they said. Just 'cause you put syrup on somethin' don't make it pancakes, they said. First they take away Christmas, they said. Now this.

That's right, folks. FAT PEOPLE KILLED JESUS.

Of course, it did not start there. The patriarchy has been fat-shaming women for at least a few hundred years, since whenever it was that being a bit chubby meant you were rich and well-fed, and therefore desirable (and why the fuck couldn't I have been born in that century?). But still? Now? What the actual fuck is wrong with everyone?! The world has gone mad.

First of all, FIRST OF ALL, size 12 is not "plus-sized." The fact that this was a "trending" discussion on most mainstream news outlets was fat-shaming at its worst. Passive-aggressive, perhaps, and disguised as "Go Gurl" empowerment—but fat-shaming nonetheless.

How must it have felt for those who really were plus-sized to know that even this literal goddess was considered so big that it was fucking NEWS that she'd be allowed to sully a magazine's bathing suit spread?

To its credit, *Sports Illustrated* has continued to feature larger-than-praying-mantis-sized models in the subsequent years, despite the backlash. Or perhaps because of it. I have a healthy mistrust of any patriarchy-licking institution suddenly changing its tune on something so polarizing unless it benefits them in some way. It must.

I do believe that, increasingly, inclusivity is good business. Some plus-sized models have actually become household names in the intervening years. But still, they are far taller and thinner than most women you'd encounter at work or on the street.

The average American woman is 5'4" and a size 16, and even she is permitted to shop in regular department stores and boutiques—yep, size 16 is the high end of a *regular* size run, where it usually sells out first—that are not relegated to the far corners of seedy strip malls, with names that conjure images of plump, middle-aged substitute teachers. Even she may buy bathing suits. Whether she has the gall to actually wear them in public to be scrutinized and assessed as Worthy or Unworthy of the privilege is another story ... I mean, would you? As witness to this never-ending unholy trinity of misogyny, objectification, and sheer cruelty, would you?

I urge you to google the *Sports Illustrated* photos of Robin Lawley that had everyone in an uproar over Fat People and their proper places. Go ahead. I'll wait.

Got it? Good.

These were the pictures that had people saying that they would boycott that year's swimsuit issue. These were the pictures that "made people sick."

There she stands: a leggy, statuesque goddess with bronzed, velvety skin and cascading waves of honeyed hair tumbling down sculpted shoulders to reveal a teeny-tiny bikini stretched over a toned, taut body that I would literally kill a kitten (OK, not literally) to inhabit for five minutes. Nary a ripple, roll, or orange rind in sight.

Have you ever seen anything so disgusting? I mean, "Curb thy foul stench, unholy minion of fruit pies!" Amirite? By the way, Robyn Lawley was also pregnant during that photo shoot.

Fat people are inferior. The message is everywhere—magazines, television, message boards, and certainly on the movie marquees. (Opening that very same weekend, in fact, was a teen comedy called *The DUFF*, an acronym for Designated Ugly Fat Friend. Everybody has one. Hilarity ensues.)

What chance do our daughters have (our mothers, our friends, ourselves) for basic self-respect, peaceful hearts and healthy minds in a world where they (we) are taught to war with our bodies at every turn, lest we become someone's DUFF? Literally zero chance, unless we actually move to Amish Country.

Even then, I imagine there is always that one fucking guy giving his buddy the old Amish side-eye—"Psst ... Brother Hezekiah, behold the bulging beneath Sister Ruth's smock this day—methinks she overindulges in thy father's farm's cheese!"

Wow, that sounded really dirty. And I actually have no idea how Amish people talk—probably not like that. I am a dick.

Now, I am no one's mother, and I think we can all agree that's for the best. But I AM an auntie—to three absolutely brilliant, kind, fierce, supermodel-stunning young women, and I hate the world on their behalf. I hate that they have ever had to wonder if they are good enough, pretty enough, thin enough, or pleasing enough to be counted. To be seen. To be valued.

I hate that when the four of us walk down the street together (NieceFest!), I can see passing men size them up like they are selecting a side of beef for their next caveman convention. *The Male Gaze.* Who in the filthy fuck decided to give this aggressively degrading eye-assault such a lovely, lyrical name? Why are we treating it like something that belongs in a fucking sonnet rather than what it is—another behavior men use to keep women in their place and reduced to body parts. It makes me want to scorch the earth beneath them.

And yet, I also hate that when those same men's eyes eventually settle on me, with my soft, middle-aged face and body, they look quickly away, clearly wishing they'd quit gawking while they were ahead.

It's a complicated feeling: I simultaneously miss the days when I was the one being leered at and loathe myself for ever assessing my own value in their despicable currency. It's a vile tug-of-war. I am insanely proud to say that all my nieces are better than this, better than me. They know their worth lies in the good they bring to the world, not in the size of their jeans.

When I was a teen in the eighties, I was "discovered" by a model scout whilst fucking around the mall with my friends, as one did in those days. I was ecstatic—certain that all the parental platitudes about my preposterous preteen height (towering over all the boys my age, having to sit in the back of classrooms in regular chairs for days while the teachers tracked down desks that would accommodate my ever-growing legs, wearing pants that began the day at the correct length but turned into "floods" by recess) were finally coming true. Eventually, my height would be an asset, they assured me; they'd be begging me to be a runway model. And it was finally happening.

I signed on with the scout's agency and began attending

weekly check-ins and "go-sees" (that's Model-ese for "job interview"), where I would inevitably be told that I was too fat. I was not fat. I was strong and healthy, and how fucking dare I sully their lobby with that bullshit? I was routinely pinched, fingerfuls of skin and connective tissue pulled away from my body in front of the other models to demonstrate my utter failure at being thin. I was put on a strict diet of brown rice and V-8 juice. I was meant to marvel at the variety afforded me; I could eat them separately! I could eat them at the same time! I could heat them up and eat them like soup! Whatever I wanted. As long as I did not surpass my calorie count (500 per day, if I recall correctly).

When even that did not result in the level of skeletal ideation I was contracted to achieve, I was told to add a daily laxative to my regimen. The awful kind. The painful kind. The doubled-over, cramps-like-stabbing, need the bathroom NOW kind. So I did. Of course I did. I did it for years. Decades, if I'm being honest. And for what? With catastrophic harm done to both my bowels and psyche that echoes to this day, the only-ever modeling job I was not deemed "too fat" for was spraying Estée Lauder perfume at unsuspecting shoppers in the same mall where they'd found me.

So who decides what "fat" is? Who gets to decide that the likes of Robyn Lawley have no business blubbering up our supermodels-only culture? To be sure, it was "groundbreaking" that there she was, bathing-suited-up in all her glorious glory, but isn't that seriously fucked-up? Were the brave execs at *Sports Illustrated* who took a gamble on this "revolution" made to suffer for their attempt to ever so slightly narrow the divide between OK and Not OK?

Did *Sports Illustrated* sales plummet? Have they suffered, long term, for moving the needle? Did anyone else "admit" to being Not Size Zero?

Hell if I know.

But one thing I do know? If Robyn Lawley is fat, then I am fucked.

And I'm having a goddamned cookie.

Won't you join me?

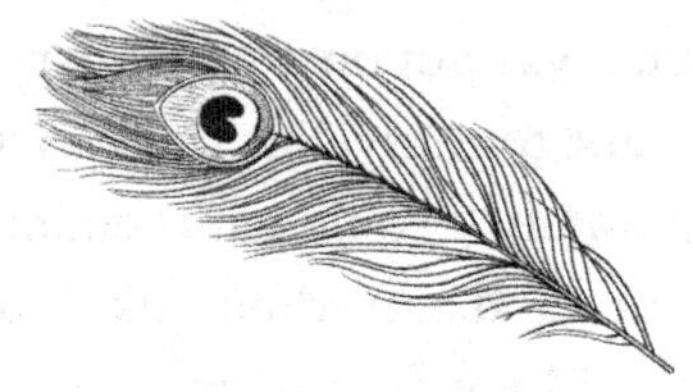

16 / the rise of the dick pic. you see what i did there

My friend, this is an emergency. A no-joke fucking crisis. The Dick Pic Problem we have, as a nation, is in Stage 5. Code Blue. Zero Fucking Hour. It has reached a fever pitch, and we are, as a species, at Peak Dick. This is not a place anyone wants to be.

Much press has been given to this issue of late, thankfully bringing to light a scourge that has been largely unrecognized by our non-single ranks for too long. I'm glad people are talking about it, writing about it, complaining about it. But the truth is, it's not doing one goddamn bit of good.

Too many of our men are broken. Even the ones who READ the articles begging them to stop sending dick pics to unsuspecting women ... they don't stop.

It might be—and I know this sounds crazy—that maybe men aren't the greatest listeners sometimes? Or that they don't particularly give a shit what we, as women, want and don't want—I know, shocking, right? They assume that their dick is special. Excluded from the advisories. Insulated by its sheer awesomeness.

My dick is magnificent, they think. *Who wouldn't want to see MY dick?*

The answer is ... *everyone*. Everyone wouldn't want to see

your dick. It is safest, gentlemen, to just go forth and accept this as gospel truth until the very moment you actually encounter someone who says, plainly, "Please, I would like to see your dick." And we will, guys. When we want to see it, we really will tell you.

What the human herd doesn't seem to realize is that this is not a new phenomenon—not some fresh outrage brought about by entitled Gen Zees who've been parented primarily by technology. Dick pics have been around as long as cameras have, and I suspect as long as dicks themselves have. I've been single, on and off, for an awfully long time—and while those old-timey rascals of last century had to be slightly more innovative in their approach to delivery, their plucky, pioneering dick-spirits prevailed. They found a way.

The difference back then—and up until very recently—is that we, as women do, *thought it was us*. That this was only happening to us because of some shameful defect or secret whore-vibe that we must be broadcasting to make guys think we wanted to see pictures of their dicks. *What is it about ME*, we asked ourselves, *that makes them think that I want this?*

We slut-shamed our own goddamn selves, for fuckssake, because the guys we liked couldn't keep their dicks in their pants and off camera. How fucked-up is that?

Nowadays, thanks to the likes of Tinder (also known as the End of Civilization), women are finally calling bullshit and starting to understand that it's not actually us. That we are not inviting the onslaught of genitalia into our unsuspecting eyeballs.

Although shaming is still a big part of the deal, it's now primarily used by men in a SUPER-clever reverse-psychology kind of way. When we do not *Ooh* and *Ahh* at the dicks, when we fail to swoon, we are immediately berated—reproached for being frigid, prudish, and (my favorite) "not as much fun as I thought." It's still *our fault*, somehow. Ever and always.

And while we endure the never-ending parade of purple-helmeted soldiers invading our personal media, we remain hyper-aware that if, GOD FORBID, we show our cellulite or bare an ankle that is anything larger in diameter than dental floss, we are chastised. We are bullied. We are revolting.

But dicks? Sure. Fire away.

Again, this discussion is not groundbreaking—it's everywhere. But what's disturbing (aside from the fact that MEN CONSTANTLY SEND US PICTURES OF THEIR PENISES) is that we women are largely portrayed as victims of the dick pic with no recourse whatsoever. Like we're not smart enough to exact any sort of revenge. (Are you kidding, motherfuckers? Revenge is what keeps us alive.)

For, let's face it, responding in kind with pictures of our own junk would hardly be taken in the spiteful spirit in which it was delivered. Because men.

Using our voices to tell them we are displeased, again, only results in petulant attempts at boomerang shame. Not one of the articles I have read offers to resolve this issue apart from tepidly using reason, entreating men to please stop. And well, we know how that goes.

Here's where I come in. I—teller of truths, warrior of women, docent of dick pics—am here to deliver this news, guys:

WE ARE MOCKING YOU.

We save them. We collect them. We show our friends. We make fun of them. We draw faces on them (sad faces, mostly). We point and laugh. We name names. We cackle uproariously at your pitiable lack of self-esteem, so thinly veiled as cock bravado. We feel a little sorry for you. We do not want to fuck you.

Because here's the thing, fellas. We will, every time, choose the guy who didn't send the dick pic—content to take our chances with what lies beneath over that which rears its ugly mushroom head. Because if it turns out you are worthy of our affections, our bodies, our time, and our love, especially—we won't fucking care what your dick looks like.

17 / boom goes the debutante

My girlfriends tend to pepper my social media feeds with superb memes depicting various displays of female power: Xena raging, lady-Vikings wielding battleaxes, Khaleesi Khaleesi-ing ... they'll say something like "This totally reminded me of you," and I'll say something like, "Hell yeah it did!" or "You too, sister!" Because I am seriously badass, right? Because I don't take shit from anyone, right? Because whoever fucks with me will be unceremoniously fileted like O-Ren Ishii by my yellow-jumpsuited *Kill Bill* awesomeness, right? Right?

Wrong.

I can get myself briefly fired up with this formidable vision of me as the ultimate No Bullshit Zone—the Powerful, Perfect Bitch. I love that vision. I love that people evidently regard me as the very last person on earth with whom they'd want to tangle, because I so desperately want to be that person.

But my enchantment is always short-lived, and I deflate rapidly as I realize that, in fact, I am exactly the person with whom you'll want to tangle. Because absolutely nothing will happen.

Chances are I won't even notice that you're being a dick-hole for the first eighty-seven or so times you decide to be a dickhole. This is a fairly serious problem, only because when I finally do notice, it means that you have pushed so far beyond the limits of decency and humanity that I completely lose my shit and the relationship is rendered unsalvageable.

I am talking about zero to blitzkrieg in the span of one well-timed dick move. Actually, I guess it would be eighty-eight. Eighty-eight dick moves. Then you're done.

So yes—I have a very high tolerance for bad behavior. I have been witness to bad behavior all my life—irrational, unpredictable, infantile behavior. Frightening behavior. Strange, inconsiderate, often cruel behavior.

At some point in my childhood it just became the new normal, and I stopped noticing. But I also realized early on that the best course of action was to do nothing—to take shelter from the storm in whatever happy place I could conjure and ride that motherfucker out. In those days my self-preservation mostly involved Sean Cassidy music and making out with my wall poster of The Fonz.

During the years I was married and stepmothering, I coped by going alone to my bedroom while the shit-pies of anarchy and defiance flew wildly about just beyond the threshold. I figured that if I just stayed behind the door, I'd never have to take one to the face. The problem, of course, was that I couldn't stay in there forever. I'd eventually run out of bourbon.

So this is what I've been working on in the never-ending business of becoming less fucked-up than I was destined to be: boundaries. Learning to stand up for myself, to speak out, to say no when I need to and to call bullshit when I smell it.

To be less accepting of bad behavior during the window of time when my NOT accepting it might still actually change its course. To fix friendships while they can still be fixed. To stop waiting to speak up until my loathing is lit with the fire of a thousand suns, by which time it's far, far too late.

It's not easy. I'm not a combative person, however much I wish I were. I will avoid the fight with every instinct that fires my soul's engine; I will avoid it like I avoid the aisle in Home Depot where the boob-looker works. Like I avoid every weird dude I was nice to once for fifteen seconds (and on a sliding scale) that now thinks we're dating.

There is nothing I dread or delay more than voicing my discontent. Rocking the boat. I don't want anyone to think I'm as crazy or reactive or irrational as the adults I watched destroy each other, and destroy me. I don't allow myself the right to anger at despicable things and despicable people because in my busted brain, that makes me the same. It makes me crazy.

So yeah, I'm working on it. Tolerating less affrontery. Calling bullshit before it becomes habit. Stepping toward the fight instead of high-tailing it away. Embracing the irony of fighting in order to save something, not destroy it.

Because while the benefits of having a very long fuse are undeniable—*I'm easy! I get along with everyone! I have low blood pressure!*—I've come to understand that anything that's left to spark and sizzle and burn that long is going to make a very big boom.

18 / we're all mad here

My friend, it's time. You've stuck with me this long, and for that, you deserve a goddamn cookie. And a cocktail. I assume you've shaken your head and muttered several dozen "WTFs" in solidarity with me throughout these pages, and for that, I am grateful. You've embraced me and my story, and as far as I'm concerned, that makes you family (I don't make the rules, dude), with all the attendant blessings and hexes that dubious honor implies. But first, you gotta meet my grampa. I think you're ready.

My mother's father: in many ways her polar opposite, but nonetheless, the certain architect of her fragile emotional edifice. She adored him and longed for his love and acceptance, which, sadly, eluded her for most of her days on this Earth (this is some circle-of-life shit happening right here, huh?). He pushed her buttons for fun, which made him an *absolute fucking legend* to us, her bubble-bound, overprotected children.

Grampa was a TRIP. (Here, I should inform you that I sometimes called him, inexplicably, Packy. No one knows why, and no one else did. It was our little secret handshake, I like to think.) To all of us kids, he was larger-than-life. Eccentric, artistic, mischievous, and more than a little terrifying if you ever found yourself on the business end of his disfavor (which I never did, obviously), he was our mighty Kong. Our patriarch. Head prankster in charge. He favored bonding activities with his grandchildren that were so outlandishly dangerous, they could have only been dreamed up to torment my poor mother. We fucking loved it.

He was a creative tinkerer, always concocting hare-brained, impetuous schemes and the accompanying vehicles required to blow shit up, launch unsuspecting grandchildren into the stratosphere, or simply take us along for whatever wild ride he was going on. Of course, we wanted IN.

At least one (possibly two) of my three broken noses happened while riding in the rickety-ass homemade wagon he built and attached to the back of his ubiquitous Cub Cadet tractor. He piled us kids (seven of us, including cousins) back there and tore around his little farm at *very unsafe speeds* (*Mom voice*), hitting the bumps hard and usually losing one or two of us over the sides or off the back of the wagon in the process.

We'd yell "Man Overboard!" and run after him and his tractor, begging him to stop so we could get back in and do it all over again. On one particular day, I had the misfortune of launching forward off the wagon and slamming face-first into the heavily chained tires of the rolling tractor. It was, of course, a bloodbath.

It was also the greatest fucking day of my life.

Grampa would frequently arm all us kids with brooms and old tennis rackets and strategically position us outside the sheep's barn when they were out grazing. Then he'd drop a stink bomb into the barn to smoke out the bats, and instruct us kiddies to swing our little hearts out and murder as many of the innocent escapees as we possibly could.

He'd pay us, too, per kill.

This particular atrocity is one I've spent my whole life trying to un-remember, and to make up for. I loved animals even then, but I loved my grampa more—I believed him when he said they were "varmints" that would make his beloved sheep sick. Now I belong to every bat conservation charity that will take my money and adopt every goddamn bat orphan I see on Instagram that needs special bat medical care. Still haven't saved more than I've murdered, I reckon.

I was an unrivaled savage. When Grampa said *Kill*, I said, giddily, *How Many*?

We had more wholesome fun, too. Playing rotten-apple baseball was another kid-favorite pastime; we'd play in the late fall, when his apple harvest was over. Grampa cut out holes in garbage bags for us to stick our little heads through and we'd wear them like ponchos. Then he'd pitch the apples to us nice and slowly, so we could smash them into a million mealy pieces. The mess was legendary.

Grampa's favorite indoor prank was bouncing the grand-kids on his knees as we jockeyed for position on his lap. One by one, he'd rapidly bounce his legs up and down and ask each of us, always, "Would I ever give you a bum steer?"

Just as we assured him that *No! He wouldn't!* he'd part his knees so we would go plummeting down, screaming in delight and horror as he caught us just before we hit the ground. He *almost* never actually dropped us.

We ate that shit up. Every time.

Of course, there was darkness in him. In the shadows, unbeknownst to us, he was profoundly haunted and likely Patient Zero in our family's legacy of mental illness. But we would not know about that until many years after he died. To us, he was simply divine. Bombastic. Swashbuckling. The joyful ringmaster of our strange circus.

There were signs, certainly.

When my brothers were very small—well before I came along—Gramps would walk with them around the idyllic, picturesque sheep farm, sharing life lessons and, occasionally, killing a rattlesnake, finding an animal skeleton, or some other heroic—and usually revolting—feat that kept the boys in thrall.

One day, when my brother Archie was around five or six, he and Gramps were hanging out together in the beautiful green swell above the farm that overlooked the pastures and my grandmother's enviable heritage flower gardens. *Pause* I need to stop here and ask you to imagine the most precious, cherubic, tow-headed little tot you can dream up in your mind. Got it? Good. Now imagine *that* kid is my brother Archie's ugly-ass friend. That's how cute Archie was.

The pastoral scene combined with Archie's cuteness to paint a picture that would make Norman Rockwell jizz his pants: early 1960s innocence. A boy and his grampa. Irreplaceable moments. Archie, a contemplative soul even at this tender age, had something on his mind.

"Gramps?" he asked, head down and idly poking a stick into the ground.

"Yep," he said.

"Are you afraid of dying?"

"Nope."

This story should have ended here, of course. But this isn't that kind of book.

"But wanna know HOW I'd like to die?" asked Grampa.

I can just see poor Archie, now sorry he'd asked the existential question that has confounded mankind since the dawn of time. He was already feeling the uh-oh vibe but was powerless to stop the conversation that he had started. I can imagine him there, adorable, wide-eyed, and terrified, *not at all* wanting to know how my grandfather wished to die.

"I want to be asleep in my bed," Grampa said.

Huh. OK. It was so … normal. So uncharacteristically peaceful and low-key. Archie relaxed a little.

"Then I want the boiler to explode in the basement. I want to be blown to bits and identified by my teeth."

Silence.

Did … that … crazy son of a bitch just … traumatize a five-year-old for life?!

Yes. Yes, he did.

My tiny, angelic brother stood there, mouth agape, clearly picturing his beloved grampa "blown to bits" and wondering what the fuck his teeth had to do with this goddamn nightmare. Gramps must have read the confusion commingled with terror in Archie's little face, so he helpfully explained that when dead bodies are so badly mutilated, dismembered, or charred that they are unrecognizable to friends and family, dental records are the only means of identifying what's left of the dearly departed.

Holy motherfucking shit.

Welp.

Remember awhile back, when I said we all came by our madness honestly? Even my mom? Yeah. This is that.

Doesn't it all make just a little more sense now?

Archie never did fully recover from this episode. He, like the rest of us, wrestles with myriad well-earned demons to this day. He keeps this particular innocence-killer locked away in a corner of his memory, in a folder marked "WHAT THE ACTUAL FUCK, GRAMPA."

I'm sure Billy has some similar memories of Gramps, but he, in particular, was simply awestruck by the wild majesty of this human asteroid.

My own relationship with Grampa wasn't quite so action-packed. I certainly got to partake in my share of perilous farm shenanigans, but overall, we shared a gentler bond.

He still managed to rescue me from some of the gloom that by that time had become pervasive in our nuclear family. He still helped me to rebel, just a little bit, only without the near-death experiences that my brothers and older cousins got to enjoy. He was older then, of course, and both his body and his spirit had begun to break down.

The best thing my Packy ever gave me was the gift of my own weirdness. He encouraged me to be silly and creative, to draw outside the lines—not things that were typically nurtured in my childhood home, where perfection was the baseline.

He helped me with homework and art projects, drove me and my cousins around in his old car with our little feet pressed up on the heating vents as we all—he included—sang ridiculous songs out the open windows in the middle of winter.

Packy once brought me a baby lamb from his farm to cuddle when I was at home sick from school, to the abject horror of my hygienically vigilant mother. He made me salt sandwiches, which my grandmother would not allow him to have, but that I would share with him gleefully, relishing the secret we shared much more than the salt sandwich. (Seriously, don't try it. It's fucking gross.)

He drove me to school each day, even though it was only three doors down from my house. Sometimes he'd take me to breakfast instead of school, where he ordered us both a dish of chocolate ice cream and nothing else.

On one occasion, around first grade, instead of school Packy and I went to the airport. He wanted me to try the best chocolate chip mint he'd ever had, which happened to be in Boston. We completed our covert mission and were home in a few hours. My mother was never the wiser; or if she was, she never said so. She let me have it.

When I was ten, my grampa died, as grampas do. For me, it was the end of the sweet and secret relief I felt in his presence, where I was simply his little Mooie, not a ticking time bomb of death and disappointment. He saw me. Unlike anyone else in my family, he really *saw* me. And he loved me anyway.

Again, the details of his illness did not come to light until long after his passing. Even then, my grandmother protected us from knowing the full truth until we were well into our adulthood. The truth about what was very likely untreated bipolar disorder; the days on end he would disappear, only to be found sitting in the dark on the floor of a hotel room all alone; the cruelty he inflicted upon my mother when she was only a girl asking to be loved; the deep fixation on his own death; the immutable unrest he carried in his soul.

The darkness that rode beside him all his life.

Knowing all this doesn't make me love him any less. It makes me sad for his suffering, and for my mother, who was ruined by it. And so on. And so on. And so on.

Generational trauma does not fuck around, y'all.

Still, I'm grateful for all of it: the broken nose(s), the explosions, the ice cream, the understanding, the sanctuary. Even the salt sandwiches.

All of it.

19 / life is a dammit rock

The story goes like this: On a family vacation long ago—back when our big, extravagant grandfather hosted big, extravagant getaways for the whole extended lot of us—we all found ourselves on some tropical island together. Barbados, maybe.

During the week we were there, the whole bunch of us would head down to the beach each morning—cousins, aunts, uncles, grandparents, nannies—and each morning, my father would trip over the very same rock on the same pathway down to the shore. And each time, he would yell, "DAMMIT!"

Every. Single. Day.

So on the last day of vacation, on our way down to the beach, my youngest cousin (three or four at the time), adorable in her sweetness to this day, called out to my father, "Uncle Bill! Watch out for the Dammit Rock!"

I think of this story often, always with a mixture of tenderness and sorrow. Because don't we all have a Dammit Rock (or two, or ten) that continues to trip us up throughout our lives? And since most of us don't have the benefit of an adorable golden-haired cherub to tell us, "Watch out for the Dammit Rock!" we continue to trip, painfully, over the same flotsam again and again.

Would we even hear her if she did?

Like my father, I am clumsy. I literally fall down, all the fucking time. Ice, dogs, shadows, rugs ... there's pretty much nothing I can't find a way to fall over. I eat spectacular shit no matter the occasion, the footwear, the familiarity of the terrain—no goddamn matter. And I almost always hurt myself, badly.

I have had at least as many X-rays as Evel Knievel and have accepted that it's only a matter of time before I begin to actually glow in the dark. Or grow one of those tiny me-twin tumors that look like goiters but are exponentially more terrifying.

The more imperative it is that I maintain grace and dignity in any situation, the more certain the odds that I will end up ass-over-teakettle on the ground, likely having opted for *commando* as the favored underwear option that day. It's all very predictable. And yet, I still put on the heels, I still forego the underpants, I still look everywhere but down when I walk—still do all the things that pretty much guarantee I will continue to single-handedly put my orthopedists' children through college.

There are other, less literal but every bit as damnable Dammit Rocks. Boys: the ones I have historically favored being too young and/or broken to possibly NOT end up crushing me. I know they're broken, I know they're dangerous, I KNOW that I'd have much better luck finding some squirrelly meth tweaker to fall in love with than a beautiful, broken, too-young boy. And yet I do it anyway. Not often. But the outcomes of these infrequent trip-ups are so dizzyingly bad that they run a pervasive course through my entire life.

It's not that I forget when the next one comes around. It's not that I don't see it. I know the Dammit Rock is there and that I will definitely fall on my face. But time after time, I fail to give a fancy fuck. I still take the same path.

Tolerating the intolerable. Fixing the unfixable. Tending, mending, managing problems that are not my own. Rescuing —people, pets, idiots, assholes ... ignoring red flags or painting them pink, with glitter! Entrusting secrets to friends I already kind of know cannot be trusted with them. Speaking before thinking. Moving to strange places and gaping, amazed, at the loneliness. Leaving my family and then aching for the comfort of them. Needing help and refusing to ask.

So very many Dammit Rocks.

Is this Human Nature? Or just my nature? Are we supposed to keep fucking the same shit up until we finally learn, by vast experience, not to? Or do we just keep clambering up and down the same rocky path forever, paying the price for our stupidity in bruises and scabs? I don't know.

The way I see it, my own options are few, and none of them particularly appealing: I can blanket my home in porn-shag and stay in my onesie forever, avoiding the perils of Outside altogether, *OR* I can pick myself up, put my heels on, aim straight for the rock, and hope to fuck I don't fall.

Or perhaps I can just learn to be more careful. Rein my shit in. Proceed with caution. Wear sensible shoes. Put on some goddamn underpants. Avoid the rocks and the strays and the love and the pain. That, I'm sure, is the answer. And it sounds perfectly awful. It sounds like defeat. It sounds like surrender. It sounds, to me, like death.

So at the risk of, well, everything—I think I'll stick to the path I know best. I'll keep falling down and fucking up until I finally get it right, or not. For better or worse, for as long as they keep making Percocet and Lifetime movies, I'll take my chances with the Dammit Rock, dammit.

20 / i hate when that happens

So, you know how, like, you're in this terrible marriage and you pretty much hate every miserable, goddamned moment of your wretched existence and you feel like you've spent forever putting up with things that no self-respecting human being would ever put up with even for a minute but you've put up with it for years and the whole sorry thing has left you so devoid of life or joy that you can't even fathom people who feel those things anymore and you wake up every single morning and tell yourself that today is The Day that you'll leave, that you'll just pack the car and grab the dogs and GO but you never do because something always comes up or you worry how you'll explain it to your judgy big brothers or you think, maybe —just maybe—if I tell the husband I'm leaving, he'll be scared enough to lose me that he will pick up his Mount Fuji of crap on the closet floor or pay a goddamned bill or tell his awful child that it is not OK to shit on the lawn but he never does, and still you try to stick it out and find things to make yourself happy but you realize you can't possibly be happy when you are allowing yourself to be used financially and abused emotionally and murdered spiritually every single day and so you finally, finally screw up the nerve to end it only to be lured back in months later by an alleged "emotional crisis" and guilted into returning to the Pit of Despair that was your life before, only this time it's even worse because the "emotional crisis" was not so much an emotional crisis as a masterclass in manipulation, and the guilting and shaming and ransacking of emails and phones and drive-by spying become daily occurrences and you find yourself begging for mercy and forgiveness just to make the crazy stop but it doesn't stop and soon you realize that the crazy has actually made you sick and now you have ulcers and you've had three teeth crumble in your mouth from all of the grinding and clenching that you don't even know you're doing and you want so badly to run away (again) but you promised to try and you really are trying but the only thing that is keeping you alive aside from the fact that your pets need you is your profound Facebook friendship with the one person who seems to truly understand and make sense of the madness and talk you out of doing anything rash and who reminds you how great you thought your husband once was and how great you were together before All This and who somehow always manages to convince you that love is worth fighting for and that surely the ulcers were caused by something else entirely and that your teeth were just exploding because, well, you're no spring chicken and if you just hang in there another day everything will be OK, and you believe your friend because you feel like friends can sometimes see things you can't and you're sure this is one of those times and one of those friends and you carry on despite the torture and the nightmares and the fact that you are drinking a LOT more bourbon than usual, which doesn't really help the ulcers but definitely helps with the getting-through until finally, finally, one day the indignity becomes too much and despite your repeated promises to "keep trying" you just can't anymore and you call it off again but that is not deemed acceptable by the other party, who decides to stalk and torment you for the next five days while you sit holed up in your house with a very big gun just waiting for a chance to use it on this motherfucker but he is so busy calling you a cunt and a whore that he doesn't give you the chance to shoot him, only to field the hundreds of texts and calls and emails calling you a cunt and a whore and you are so grateful to your special Facebook friend, who is helping you through this yet again, and you feel like you can tell him anything and that your secrets and rage and heart-break are safe with him because you trust him implicitly, and since he is the one friend who has seen you through the whole miserable breakup from start to finish you know you don't really have to explain anything and that he will understand why you had to do what you did—why you had to go, again—why you are getting off the hamster wheel and getting the hell out of Dodge and getting the fuck out of the marriage, and you know your friend won't judge you even though he does not agree with your decision because, well, that's the kind of friend he is, and when you have finally extricated yourself from the poisonous sham of a union and cut the cord that tied you to all that pain and torment, you feel exhilarated because the cancer is gone once and for all and you think nothing could possibly hurt you ever again now that you are free and everything is swell, right up until the part when your special friend reveals to you that he is actually your husband pretending to be someone else and that he has spent the past year weaving this elaborate web of deception and using this fake identity to stalk you and commit emotional espionage on you, and the whole time you were trying to reconcile, he looked you in the eye and lied and deceived you again and again and led two lives and kept them immaculately separate from each other and you never had a fucking clue, so now you feel like the biggest asshole the world has ever made and you wonder how you could be so stupid and you are embarrassed because you were so handily duped but you are also sad because now you've lost the friend you trusted and you realize that your entire life has been turned upside down by duplicity and betrayal and you don't even trust yourself to order a sandwich anymore because maybe the sandwich is pretending to be some other kind of sandwich behind your back, but then you realize you sound completely fucking mad and that you're not actually fit for human company right now and maybe you'd better just take your weird imposter-sandwich and go back to bed for a while, like, say, six-ish months and ***never ever*** speak of it, because you can't, until you can—and then you can speak of nothing else because you are so completely fucking broken by it all?

No? Oh. Me neither.

When I first shared the above story as a blog post, hooooo-boy ...

What followed was an epic shitstorm. Lines were drawn, double-dealers exposed, martyrs and hypocrites drawn out, friendships lost and broken. I was accused of launching a vicious "attack" upon the former stepson, and in truth, I have questioned my judgment and motive for bringing him into the retelling at all.

First, to those who've deemed me cruel and inhuman for exposing this labyrinthine saga and its wily players to my tiny circle of readers, I say this: Call me when your husband fashions an elaborate ploy to stalk and spy on you with a fake identity. Call me when some kid comes along and shits on your lawn and on your life. Call me when the betrayal finally beats you, and when everything you think you know is a lie. Then we'll talk.

In the meantime, kindly fuck off.

This sideshow was my life—not a day or a week or a moment. My LIFE. For years. Shaming me for *telling* the horrible things doesn't magically excuse or erase the horrible things. It doesn't work that way, to the great dismay of blame-deflectors everywhere. This is my story, and I don't feel compelled to apologize or defend myself for telling it. Everything I said was true. And plenty more that I didn't say—that I wouldn't.

To Clarify: Primarily, I am not angry anymore. Really. I mean, don't get me wrong: I still loathe this monster with all of my being, and writing or talking about it never fails to whip up my hatred. But those moments of abject rage and unthinkable betrayal I wrote about in the previous section, they were only moments.

They are gone now.

I am not still reeling. Nor am I driven by any sort of lust for vengeance. My feeling on that subject is simple: Go Bobbit or Go Home. I went home. To my laptop. And wrote. Well, actually I went home to my couch and stayed there in a PTSD, carbs, and Valium coma for many months before I was even able to talk about it.

But then, I wrote.

I did not create that post in order to hurt anyone or "expose" my ex-husband as an emotional abuser or raving lunatic—trust me, he does not need my help in doing so. I wrote it to get it out, and indeed, it was a fantastic purge. But as far as I knew, anyone reading my minor-league musings was either a friend or family member and likely already knew the story.

My blog had almost no subscribers. Never did I imagine the breadth and scope of readers that would find their way to that post on that day and enter the swirling brown vortex of doom that was my marriage and its Lifetime-worthy demise.

Second, I am no one's bitch, and no one's victim. If there's anything I AM still angry about, it's that ***I allowed this to happen***.

It was with my total permission that my ex-husband and his son treated me with unconscionable disrespect, lived off of me without contribution, drained my resources, and turned my home into a festering pit of refuse and despair. I allowed it. Every single day that I bellowed or cried or begged or threatened but didn't leave, I allowed it. And in doing so, I asked for more.

I knew what I was getting when I married them (make no mistake, potential steps—it's a package deal); this was not a post-wedding Worst Surprise Ever. I was not tricked or duped into thinking I was getting some great deal—I knew exactly what I was in for, and for me to expect different behaviors from my former husband and his son would have been like adopting a mastodon and then being outraged because it broke my house. Of course it did. It's a fucking mastodon.

The fault is mine. I invited the chaos into my life, drew it a hot bath, gave it the guest room, and handed over my credit card.

My job, now, is to figure out why I thought it was OK for as long as I did. Why I stayed, why I thought I deserved it. Why it took an unfathomable show of treachery for me to finally leave. Why I brought home that goddamned mastodon.

I'm making some progress there. I imagine if you've read this far, you too can piece together the pathology of my damage. It doesn't take a fucking master sleuth.

To Observe: Many, many more people than I realized have

endured similar torment. I had no idea. I heard from several women who have been stalked, "taken," frightened, used, bullied, deceived, some even beaten—stories much worse than mine.

They were afraid or embarrassed or ashamed to talk about it, and thanked me for being impertinent enough to tell my story publicly, as if by doing so I was also telling theirs. I am OK with that, speaking the Secrets of the Douchey Exes Sisterhood. And I would please like Cameron Diaz to play me in the movie. I'll need a breezy sidekick.

How did so many strangers find my post? Likes and shares, that's how. And I had virtually no audience; I cannot stress this enough. What does this say? Sure, people love a trainwreck, but I think it's more than that.

I think it's partly that those who sometimes worry their lives have entered the dreaded Realm of the Mundane can dip their toes, ever so briefly, into the cesspool of deception and espionage and drama and dysfunction of such a tale and quickly run back to the safety of their lives and families, grateful for their certainties and permanence. People who have beachfront property at said cesspool, like me, read because we like to know that we're not alone, and that maybe someone else really does understand, and that maybe we can laugh about it together someday. Or cry, or scream, or even better—move to the suburbs.

But mostly, I think it's because people truly care about others' struggles. (I know, very off-brand.) And because we can frolic together on Insta and play Words With Friends and meet for drinks and go to festivals and work side by side with people we truly care about, and have no idea what lies beneath. What they're going through, where they've been, what they've survived, what they don't tell.

As for me, I am mostly glad I told. It came at a price, to be sure, but I have to believe the gift outweighs the cost. To have told the tale is to be free of it. And that's way better than a pet mastodon.

21 / in a shocking twist, my neighbors suck

Honestly, it didn't start out this way. Once free of my repugnant marriage, I moved back to Park City and into this idyllic enclave with wide-eyed wonderment and childlike longing for the kind of neighborly closeness and camaraderie that I knew was possible from my fierce devotion to *Melrose Place* in the early nineties (yes, the classic years: post–Amy Locane, pre–Lisa Rinna. Bitch, please).

That's right. I did not come in with guns blazing, à la Amanda Woodward—plus I could never get a handle on that awesome overbleached, messy sex-hair she rocked, no matter how I tried; it would've really added a soupçon of drama to my struggle.

Nay, I fancied myself more the Matt Fielding of this strange new Utopia ... the gentle, humble, selfless, quiet, gay social worker that everyone would root for (granted, I am neither gentle, nor humble, nor selfless, nor quiet, nor gay, nor a social worker—but this is my book, dammit).

I was nice to everyone. Warm. Complimentary. Hospitable, even—inviting virtual strangers to "drop by anytime," which, as you can probably gather, is a torture akin to eyeball acupuncture for yours truly. But determined as I was to live in harmony among my peers (because let's face it, chaos can't stop lovin' me), I floated in upon gossamer wings—a peaceful pixie angel alighting in a limpid pool of unicorn tears, my goodness beaming brightly upon my neighbors like so much disco glitter. It was fucking exhausting.

And indeed, several months went by before the trouble started. In fairness, it was likely because it was the middle of a Utah winter and I was hobbled by a broken foot, emotionally leveled by unfathomable personal deception, and wallowing in self-loathing misery most of that time. Translation: I never left the house, and thus had very little opportunity to offend anyone (it's a numbers game with me).

But when spring rolled around, I slowly began to dip my newly un-casted toe in the pool of the living once again—strolling the neighborhood with my responsibly leashed dogs[1] while making dramatic, exaggerated shows of picking up their poo and jauntily dangling the full shit-sacs for all to see as I made my rounds, lest anyone think me inconsiderate or cavalier. I made it clear that I was no one's shit pirate.

So imagine my surprise when, one summer evening, I passed the usual driveway kegger raging on my street (six drunk, fat dudes in plastic chairs, poised to scout the local talent; it was SUPER classy) and, bracing myself for the usual grunts and nudges of Cro-Magnon-esque appreciation that, as a woman, I ~~live for~~ expect and upon which I base my ~~entire self-worth~~ unblemished moral superiority, was met instead with the following: "Oh, is that the BAD neighbor?"

What. The. Fuck. Bro.

Surely there was some mistake. And I happen to know I

---

1. In fact, my leashes and poo-bags and muzzles singled me out as a priggish Mrs. Grundy—smugly parading my prissy ass about like a bustled Victorian school marm who got lost at a Vegas piercing convention. Leashes? Totally uncool, turns out. Talk about a goddamned backfire.

was having a good ass day—I mean, certainly worth a mention from some drunk fat dudes, anyway. They were simply referring to someone else. Right?

I successfully deluded myself until the following evening, when, on my walk—clear on the other side of the development, far from the driveway dickholes—I encountered a swingy-skinned middle-aged-plus woman skipping down the road with her wildly age-inappropriate attire and loose, deranged dog, and asked her politely if she could leash or grab him as we passed. I was with my Malamute at the time, who was dog-aggressive. She was also supremely clever, and when her murder-gene was activated, there was no harness, muzzle, leash, or prison that could keep her from getting to her prey. Loose dogs were my absolute nightmare. So I asked her nicely to hold her dog. Which she did, but made sure to also hiss at me ominously, "EVERYBODY KNOWS ABOUT YOU ..."

First of all, harpy, *super*-sexy bucket hat (said no one, ever). And secondly, HUH? What is it that everyone knows? I had no voice to question her, so great was my shock. But it got me thinking. *What DO they know?* Seriously.

As I did a mental rundown of likely personal infractions, my panic mounted in proportion to the list of possibilities ... Did they know about my unrelenting, party-lines-be-damned crush on George W. Bush?

Did they know that I almost never washed the pot after I made pasta?

Did they know that my boobs were fake?

Did they know that I watched the Disney *Halloweentown* movies at least once a month, year-round, and that they comforted me, unfailingly?

Did they know that I used to collect little pieces of foot skin as a child and keep them in a lavender velour box, sometimes snacking on them months later? (Hey, don't knock it till you try it—it did not always feel safe to leave my room to find a snack, and anyway, that shit is delicious.)

Did they know that I groom my lady parts sunny-side up on the living room floor so I can watch *Vampire Diaries* concurrently and imagine that one (fine, both—who am I kidding?) of the undead teen Salvatore brothers might come along and make the sadistic agony of undercarriage waxing, like, totally worth it?

Did they know that when my doorbell rang, I always pretended I wasn't home?

Did they know that if I was sick or sad, I sometimes blew my nose in my shirt if the tissues were too far away?

Did they know that my heart was perfectly fucking broken because I missed my chance to have children?

Did they know that when my cat gently kissed my eyelids, the sweetness of it made me cry?

Did they know that despite all my posturing and profanity, I truly and profoundly cared what they thought of me?

Meh. Probably not.

But whatever it is they did "know," these neighbors of mine, I considered myself royally rogered. And somewhat unfairly judged, I'm not gonna lie.

I truly still have no idea what could have possibly earned me the title of The Bad Neighbor.

But I did know, with certainty, that the only choice or chance I had was to whip up some crazy sex-hair, open a can of Amanda Woodward–Certified Whoop-Ass up in this heezy, and sit my Jersey ass down on the Iron Fucking Throne of Neighborhood Drama, its reluctant—but reigning—queen.

So bring it, bitches. I know where you live.

22 / the only advice you will ever need. like, ever

THAT'S RIGHT, FRIENDS. Your horny, half-witted, humble-ish, eighth-favorite asshole is in possession of the ONE SINGLE THING you need to know in order to fully participate, winningly, in life.

I realize that sounds like a bold claim, but I promise you, it's true. There really *is* a secret to life, and I am going to tell it to you. There really *is* only one thing you need to do to change your entire fucking existence. Are you ready? Here it is—The Only Advice You Will Ever Need:

Don't be a dick.

That's it. It's so simple, and everyone thinks they already know it, but they do not. There is never a time, a situation, or a problem that cannot be solved by simply making the choice, right then and there, to NOT be a dick. You will never go wrong.

"But, Marie," you cry, "surely you cannot solve all of my problems with just that one little thing ..."

Yes. Yes, I can.

This directive will never fail you. This is the *I Ching*. The Mothership. The Holy Fucking Grail of unsolicited advice. If everyone on earth did just this one thing, there would be no war. There would be no divorce, there would be no hunger, poverty, racism, homophobia, or child abuse. There would be no bullying. No crime. None.

If every person, every day, in every quandary, faced their choices with the simple aim of Not Being a Dick, just imagine how different things would be. Here are some examples (numbered for your convenience), in case you are finding this shit hard to follow:

1. I'm in a hurry, and the only parking spot left at the gym is handicapped parking: Should I take the spot? (Because seriously, like, are any handicapped people REALLY going to come to the gym in the forty-five minutes it might take me to go prance around in my Spandex, flirt with some meatheads, drink a smoothie, and not work out?) *No. You should not take the handicapped spot. Don't be a dick.*
2. I don't want to vaccinate my children because I think I know better than a century of doctors and scientists, and I want to start wielding the tight fist of parental control over my kids as early as possible by gambling with, oh, I don't know, their health, and I don't really give a shit whether their pure, unvaccinated asses make everyone else in the entire fucking world sick. What should I do? *Vaccinate your fucking kid. Don't be a dick.*
3. I'm kinda seeing this girl/guy/whatever, but I've lost interest and I don't really feel like explaining myself or risking a scene, so is it OK if I just disappear into the ether and never call or text her/him/whatever again? *No. It's not OK. Find some*

humane way to let her/him/ whatever know that you won't be calling again. Don't be a dick.

4. Should I tip the movers/server/cab driver/etc.? *Yes. Don't be a dick.*
5. Should I take up two parking spots at the crowded mall, since my car is so much nicer than all of the other ones? *No. Don't be a dick.*
6. My country is hosting the Olympics and I'd like to make sure that gay people know they are unwelcome in my land because gay people are obviously (a) pedophiles and (b) criminals and (c) will definitely brainwash our 100% heterosexual children to join the Gay Side. May I ban homosexuals from my country? *No. Don't be a dick.*
7. Should I blow up an airplane or festival full of people because it will score me some big points and a few virgins in the afterlife? *Dude, no. Don't be a dick.*
8. I make a lot of money. Should I have to share it with the less fortunate or pay more taxes to help ensure that each human being in our country has their basic needs taken care of? *Yes. Don't be a dick.*
9. I'm thinking about spying on my wife. Should I make up a fake Facebook profile and go to elaborate lengths to trick her into thinking I'm someone else in order to extract information out of her? *No. You should not do that. Don't be a dick.*
10. My beautiful yellow-haired God-fearing daughter wants to get married to a [insert racial, religious, or ethnic inconvenience here]. Can I stop her? *No, you cannot. Don't be a dick.*
11. I'm dating two people at once, and they both think that we're exclusive ... can I continue on like this

indefinitely, 'cause it's pretty fucking awesome? *No. Pick one. Don't be a dick.*

12. Should I call someone fat or ugly because I secretly loathe myself and being mean makes me feel important? *No. You should not. Don't be a dick.*
13. I think my husband is cheating on me with his secretary. Should I send her a dead bunny? *No. You should, however, find yourself a forest witch and ask her to curse your cheating husband with an overactive conscience and involuntary honesty (and maybe some persistent genital odor), then divorce his sorry ass when he confesses. But you should still not be a dick.*

Do you SEE, my friends? How easy? There are always, always, two very simple choices. To be (a dick), or not to be (a dick.) That is the question; the only question. And I'm giving you the answer.

Don't Be a Dick. Ever.

The choice is virtually never ambiguous or "complicated" (which, let's face it, is just Asshole-ese for "I am not willing to make a choice," also known as Being a Dick). I personally guarantee that if YOU make a conscious and focused effort to Not Be a Dick, others will follow. Because Being a Dick feeds on itself—it perpetuates the dickery and spreads it throughout society like an unvaccinated toddler with their medieval fucking swamp measles. When you stop Being a Dick, people around you and affected by you won't need to Be a Dick either, and they will stop, too. It's magic. Like a beautiful, twinkly, dickless unicorn spreading peace and kindness throughout the land. Fine, it's *probably* just cheap glitter. But it's still a magical dickless unicorn, so you shut right up. That shit is so sparkly.

So that's all. The Secret of Life. It's the only thing you ever need to know and the only thing you ever need to teach your children. So what's it going to be? Do you want to be the swamp measles or the unicorn glitter?

Pick the glitter. Don't be a dick.

23 / i drank the kool-aid. and it was goddamned delicious. ok?

Judge me all you want for my grown-up love of Justin Bieber. Seriously. I don't care. Do it. But while you're judging me, ask yourself this: Is it because you secretly love him too and you totally wish you were a preteen girl so you could justify your love, Madonna-style? Or is it because you are a self-righteous, self-professed music snob looking for places to leg-lift your disdain, and what better fire hydrant than the adorable teen sensation who won over the world with his awesome hair and mad pop chops? Thought so.

Admittedly, I only first knew about the Biebs because of my three dear nieces, and my single most heart-exploding-with-joy memory is of driving with them in my car and singing "Baby" together over and over at the top of our lungs. Truly. Nothing in this world can make me feel gladder or better or brighter than *that* memory, and hearing the song brings that joy back to me here in the present moment, where, let's be honest, it doesn't frequent much these days ... *and the only reason I have that memory is because of Justin Bieber.*

I have driven around in the car scream-singing with my nieces for thirty-plus years and have never had any other artist or song or moment feature so prominently in a picture of pure, captured happiness. That's right. Justin Bieber gave me a joy tattoo.

Which is why I leapt at the chance to take my youngest niece to his concert in Miami a few years ago. It was more selfish than noble, although I totally played the "Aren't I a martyr?" card when chronicling my four-thousand-mile journey to the jumbotron and back for sympathetic friends. Niece #3 missed out on the NSYNC/Backstreet/Xtina outings that I got to share with the older girls a decade or so earlier, and I wanted a moment like that with her. I wanted to bond with her over something she loved, as I had gotten to do with the others. Also, I wanted her to think I was awesome. Obviously.

I cannot lie—the night was dark and filled with more than a few terrors. Primarily, the enormous, flagrant signage everywhere in and around the arena announcing Bacardi as the North American sponsor of JB's tour. Nice. Pimping booze to kids not nearly old enough to even drink it illicitly at forbidden high school parties—to kids who will endure years of anti-alcohol diatribes from parents who ignore the irony of railing against the very thing that delivered the single greatest thing in their world (aka the Biebs) to their very doorstep. Try unconfusing those ~~future alcoholics~~ kids. I dare you.

I'm pretty sure that, at the time, Justin himself was not even old enough to drink. This actually blows my mind, and I am in no way prudish or ignorant of the shit that teens get up to. It just reeks of the kind of tone-deaf capitalism that will forever furnish astute comedians with fresh material.

However, when the Biebs himself finally emerged, my every last remnant of snark and judgment dissolved. I didn't even mind so much about the eardrums. Totally worth it. Both for the joy on my niece's face and for the simple fact that Justin

Bieber is a STAR. Which was never more evident than when seeing him do his Bieber thing after we had endured not one, but two horrifically bland opening acts.

Those boys could sing, too—maybe even better than JB. They could also dance and show us their teen muscles and mug for the cameras with the best of them. But they were not stars. They will never have a fever named after them. Not ever.

I used to think it was just the hair. Which, by the way, is magnificent. I mean, the iconic Bieber coif is obviously an architectural triumph—duh—but it is also a lovingly sculpted nonpareil erected by tiny frenzy-fairies using an unguent of Aphrodite tears and magical gumdrops made from the still-beating hearts of baby unicorns. It's that good. You cannot take your eyes off it—not that you'd want to.

I do, however, admit to recoiling with awkward embarrassment the moment that this tiny wonder removed his shirt to reveal the hairless boy-torso beneath. I actually did look away for that—I had to. I mean, I'm as pervy as the next guy (oh, who am I kidding, I'm exponentially more pervy than the next guy, and the guy after that), but seeing those ripped baby-abs—like a six-pack made of Go-Gurt—made me feel icky inside. Which is actually kind of a relief, if you want to know the truth.

So there. I said it. I love Justin Bieber (fully clothed) and I don't care who knows it. I also don't care that you and everyone you know hates him, or why you hate him, or that you now hate me. I love him for the mosaic of joyful memories he's become a part of and the happiness those memories conjure. For the thrill he gave my niece and for the bliss of being there with her to see it.

Say what you want—this li'l dude is a supernova. He possesses a radiance and a spark and a gift that mere mortals do not have and could not channel if they did. It's not about the hair. It's not about the Bacardi or the girls or the dumb pants. It's not about being the best singer, or the best dancer, or the best musician.

It's about being The Biebs.

And that is all you need to know.

24 / merry fucking christmas

Each year, inevitably, the onslaught begins earlier. Department stores and television ads start heralding the Christmas season with glittering balls of mandatory joy accompanied by super-fucking-offensive religious music around mid-fall, by my estimation. I barely get to drink ~~the blood of my enemies~~ my festive Witches Brew before I start hearing about ol' Baby Jesus and his miraculous "virgin" birth (wink, wink, sister Mary ... I see you). Other winter holidays, like Hanukkah and Kwanzaa, get some rudimentary props, but let's face it, Jesus is the star of this show whether you like it or not.

Personally, I'd like to normalize my Welsh ancestors' tradition of Mari Lwyd, wherein Yule-fueled revelers place a horse's skull over their own, bedeck it with ribbons and baubles, and place colorful glass balls in its empty, cavernous eye sockets. Then they drape the whole horrifying ensemble in a sackcloth and show up at their neighbors' front doors to initiate an epic rap battle, which, if the homeowner loses, means they have to let the terrifying dead holiday horse inside.

God, I love my people.

But since America is literally no fun at all, we get Jesus. So much Jesus. You can't escape it—no one can—so here's my suggestion: Don't even try. I'm here to help.

If you're like me, and since you're still reading this book, you probably are—you don't take kindly to anyone imposing seasonal gladness on you where there is more likely tepid apathy at best, and at worst, slow-simmering grief, unbearable loneliness, or quiet desperation.

If you're like me, you wonder what's wrong with you that you don't feel it—that magic that everyone talks about and that sells a trillion dollars' worth of plastic shit that people will still be paying for NEXT Christmas, and the next.

If you're like me, you want to sit quietly with your thoughts —and maybe some goddamn twinkle lights for ambience, because have you ever tried to casually acquire a horse skull in this hellhole?—and reflect on why this time of year makes everyone pretend to be so happy when surely you can't be the only one to feel so fucking sad.

I am pretty clear on my own holiday triggers, but knowing why they kill you doesn't ever stop them from killing you. The death of my boyfriend in a car crash thirty years ago, Dec 12th; each year a fresh cut, in spite of the fading color of the memory. Old pain from the sudden, unfathomable loss. New pain from the slow forgetting of it.

My grandpa died on December 10th in 1978—but I replay the moment again and again: a child's first real dose of death with no idea of what it really means or how it will hurt forever. To this day, I see them leave for the funeral, which I was not allowed to attend; I hear my mother's wails of grief for her dead father in my ears even still.

My birthday, December 18th. Looming mortality. Aging skin, lost youth, aching joints. Crushing disappointment. The hourglass sand, silently slinking downward.

Worst of all, each December I inevitably encounter the Christmas china I began collecting in my twenties for the family I so cavalierly assumed I'd someday have. Little sets for Santa's milk and cookies that I imagined my babies and I would fill with goodies and leave by the hearth on so many Christmas Eves.

But there are no children. There is no family. And every year when I open the hutch and see the ghosts of those dream babies in the tiny cups and saucers, it is a fresh kick in the cunt. A sucker punch to a wasted womb. Every year, I am reminded that my family's generations of holiday traditions and memories will die with me for lack of progeny. Every year, I know it's coming. And every year, it doesn't matter.

So this year, I am putting my seasonal misery to good use. For you, my friend. I've compiled a very important compendium of advice to hopefully make your holidays somewhat less godawful. Things you should definitely do or not do. Fucks you shouldn't ever give. Shit you should never, ever drink (hint: eggnog). Here goes.

My Foolproof Plan for Having a Less Sucky Holiday

MFC Rule #1: Ignore every single article you see on "How to Stay Slim This Holiday Season." Fuck. That. Shit. No one is gonna make me suffer through the worst of what the holidays have to offer (see above, plus terrifying seasonal attire, mandatory office parties, maxed-out credit cards, and very little daylight) without at least taking the edge off with some goddamn delicious Yule log. What's that? You want me to eat my dinner of lettuce and dry chicken breast *before* I go to the party so that I'm not hungry when I get there? And drink half of a watered-down wine spritzer for a low-cal but peer-pressure-proof holiday toast?

Riiiiiggggghhhhttt.

WHY THE FUCK WOULD I EVEN GO TO THIS FUCKING PARTY IF NOT FOR THE FUCKING BOOZE AND COOKIES, YOU FUCKING MANIAC?

MFC Rule #2: Don't make New Year's resolutions. I can't believe I even have to tell you this. Resolutions are just one more opportunity for you to inevitably fail yourself. Spare yourself the swirling vortex of self-loathing you will feel when you do not lose thirty pounds by Memorial Day. Or worse, when you quit even trying by two weeks into next year. Trust me on this. You will "juice" exactly three times before you realize that it makes a huge fucking mess and tastes disgusting and gives you explosive diarrhea and costs $47 in wild-crafted organic produce to make ¼ cup of pulpy brown "juice" that looks and tastes exactly like the stuff you just sharted into your underpants because no one told you about juice farts. Buy some goddamn V8. You're welcome.

Seriously—if you truly need or want to make a meaningful change or two in your life, do it slowly, on your terms, with proper professional and personal support to ensure you'll succeed at whatever it is. Don't put it off or start before you're ready on some arbitrary date that society has deemed The Time. Fuck society.

MFC Rule #3: Don't let anyone tell you what you need. Only you know what you need. If you've had a terrible year and you want to spend Christmas or Hanukkah or Kwanzaa by yourself to just process that shit so you can move on from it sooner? Then you spend it by yourself. You are not obligated to fulfill anyone's outreach quota by agreeing to spend your holiday doing something you don't want to do with people you don't want to do it with just because traditional wisdom has decided that no one should be alone for the holidays. Who makes this shit up? Sometimes that's exactly what you need. Listen to your own voice.

MC Rule #4: Please, for the love of GAWD, do not watch *It's a Wonderful Life* or *Miracle on 34th Street* or any other of their "classic" ilk. You will cry. You will wonder where your life went wrong. You will ache for all of the things that you thought you'd have and don't, and for the lost promise of your long-gone childhood. You will feel worse than you did before you spent two hours of your life watching it. Two hours of your life you'll never get back. Two hours of your life you could have spent watching a holiday movie on Lifetime featuring Steve Guttenberg as a single Santa lookin' for love. Now that shit? Is uplifting.

MFC Rule #5: Don't buy presents for everyone you know. Seriously. Most of those people will not get you anything. You'll feel bad, they'll feel bad. You'll be broke and resentful. And then the next year you'll be like, "Fuck that, I'm not getting her anything this year because she didn't get me anything last year," and she's like, "Well, fuck, I'd better get her something this year because she got me something last year," and the whole cycle of you both cocking it up will go on for years.

Talk to your friends and family before the holidays and decide if you're exchanging gifts. Pick a Secret Santa. Decide to do something together instead of buying some dumb shit nobody needs or wants. Just have it figured out before embarrassing yourself and others.

MFC Rule #6: DO buy gifts for yourself. A soft new sweater. A mani/pedi. An awesome steak dinner in which you wouldn't normally indulge. Anything to soothe yourself during this wretched, emotional *Titanic* of a season. Treat yourself kindly. You are doing the best you can—and sure, it will never be nearly enough to please everyone or even yourself. That's OK. Appreciate yourself for trying. And for the burdens that you bear. Always remember that other people have problems that are far worse than yours, but never diminish your own in so doing. Buy yourself a gift that will remind you that you are fucking awesome even when you don't feel like you are.

MFC Rule #7: Don't look in people's windows, either literally or figuratively. It's not just creepy, it's dangerous. You may see scenes from a life you wish you had—a tree loaded with presents beneath it, joyful children, parties featuring merry-making by people who actually seem merry (the real story, of course, is that the husband is cheating and the wife is popping pills and the kids are entitled little fucks who will grow up to be terrible people, so don't let the life-glitter fool you) ... or worse, you may see an old person eating a TV dinner all alone in a Barcalounger, and then you will really want to kill yourself.

Trust me. Do not try to compare your life or experience with anyone else's. Head down, eyes on the ground. You don't want to know—nay, you CAN'T know—what's going on in there. Save yourself some goddamn anguish and don't even try.

There you have it. My foolproof plan for Having a Less Sucky Holiday. I hope it helps you. Now, if you'll excuse me, I have some fucking Pfeffernüsse to eat while I hit the dark web.

searches horse skulls

25 / talk derby to me

Once the emotional fallout from my ex-husband's obscene misdeeds began to subside, I found myself in a state of numb inertia that I couldn't seem to shake off.

I lived in the sweet embrace of my couch. I stared at nothing. I doubted everything. I was half a human. Alive but not living. I knew that something had to change, but I felt so powerless, so defeated and small, that I couldn't imagine doing the work it might take to move past what had happened. To find the thing that would save me from myself—because I was doing a shit job of it on my own.

I was out of ideas. I had tried therapy, yoga, meditation, chakra cleansing. (STFU. I was desperate.) In addition to the marital PTSD, I'd lived through five years of debilitating illness and several sudden deaths in a short time ... I was simply crippled by grief and defeat. But I was also tired of feeling powerless, beaten, afraid. I lay around limply and scoured my imagination for the most outlandish precedent of female badassery I could conjure.

I toyed with the idea of martial arts, but it didn't thrill me. The enemy-pummeling was too ... hypothetical for my taste. I needed to exorcise the slow-death demon that was animating my meat suit and simultaneously draining the life from it. I needed something bigger.

Then, one day, there it was. It hit me like an AC unit toppling out a tenth-story window onto the city sidewalk below.

Roller derby.

DEAR GOD, I AM A FUCKING GENIUS. That I had never roller-skated in my life seemed less important than the sudden, blinding flash of my own brilliance. I would do it. There was no one left to stop me.

And that was it. I immediately found a league, signed up for their Fresh Meat boot camp, and knew with absolute certainty that this was what I had been waiting for. I'd have to learn how to roller-skate, of course (my mother believed roller-skating was for "fast girls" and the local roller rink was a hotbed of masher activity, so I was not allowed to go there as a child), but that seemed trivial compared to the overarching triumph of my decision.

So I spent most of the winter between 2012 and 2013 getting my ass kicked. Really fucking hard. Because that's exactly what I signed up for. That's exactly what I wanted, and *EXACTLY* what I needed. That's right, y'all. Your mild-mannered, people-hating, underachieving eighth-favorite asshole ever was now a goddamned, bona fide roller girl.

But this chapter is not really about me, so much. Actually, it totally is. But it's also about the magnificent, indestructible, stunningly beautiful women who came into my life, or came closer, when I began this awesome ridiculousness. Fierce women. Kind women. Women who taught me about things like "'giner shiners" and "stripper stretches."

WHERE HAD THESE PEOPLE BEEN ALL MY LIFE?

In the most bizarre way, that blood-splattered track became my home, my church, my shrink, my PLACE. And I shared that track with a large handful of women who felt exactly the same way.

Clearly, I cannot speak for all derby girls, nor do I presume to know everyone's story ... but I know my own, and I know my friends' stories, and I know why WE were there. It wasn't for the 'giner shiners, folks. Ouch, by the way. *Ouch.*

We were there because we were broken. Beautifully, crushingly, perfectly broken. Busted right the fuck up. And the other ways we'd tried to put ourselves back together had failed, or fallen short. We'd tried "healing," we'd tried breathing, we'd tried forgiveness ... not to mention yoga, therapy, meditation, hiking, knitting, the "high road," booze, food, weed, teen vampires (did I say that, or did I think it?)—you name it. We'd tried it. And we all came to the same conclusion: Sometimes all that's left to do is just to kick some goddamn ass. And that's what we'd come to do. We'd come to Break It Forward. And in doing so, to put ourselves back together.

My fellow skaters and I sported names like Bruiser Ego, Veronica Tastrophe, Barb Dwyer, Decks-Her Morgan, Crystal Brawl, and Waste Management (that's mine, a touching homage to my home state and its pesky habit of hiding bodies in garbage dumps). Power names; names that gave us permission to bust asses and to advertise our intentions to do so. Explosive, violent, unhinged names that allowed us to embrace those undainty elements and celebrate them.

By the way, 'tis a gross miscarriage of nickname justice that the best ones always go to the MTV miscreants—I refer, of course, to The Situation. The Rolls-Royce of nicknames—especially when, before derby, the best I ever did was Laverne 2000 after a brief mid-nineties flirtation with monograms and sassy back talk. Waste is better. Waste takes out the fucking trash.

These were our true selves. Every woman should have a derby name, whether or not she ever puts on a pair of skates.

Every single goddamned woman. We've all got a roller girl inside of us, but most of us don't know it yet—we won't know until we need her. It's how we *should* see ourselves, and sometimes, how we MUST see ourselves. Because let's face it, when the shit hits the fan, who're you gonna call, Susie Sunshine? Or Armageddon Furious? Thought so.

Again, I cannot know how each of us found derby, or how *it* found us. But my theory is that most of us ended up here because we had to. (Please keep in mind, I also once had a theory that if I gave enough "thought energy" to Jordan Catalano, he would magically become real, and also my boyfriend—but whatevs. This one's better.) Because, thanks to some past hurt, or hoax, or heartbreak, we had been stripped of our power, and we wanted it the fuck back.

One day after practice, two of my friends and I sat—tired, sweating, and so, so happy—removing our safety gear and chatting about some move we were trying to perfect, when one of them said, "Wow. This is a bench full of broken bitches."

That shit hit deep. Profound and perfect and true. There we sat together: Heartbreak, Betrayal, Mayhem—not our derby names, but they certainly could have been ... the worst that life had to offer—helping each other to kick those things' asses right back to where they came from (usually, that place has a penis, but I digress).

Making the best of the worst, and doing it together. Putting back the broken pieces and making something stronger and far more beautiful than the original. Digging deep and pushing through (and if you were me, taking out anyone who got in your way, mostly because you didn't know how to stop yet) and doing it for yourself. Or in spite of yourself. What-the-fuck-EVER. Doing it. Just ... doing it.

I spent several months nestling into a makeshift, homemade traction device after each practice, with ice packs on both knees, moist heat on my ass (Nothing to do with derby, that—just, who doesn't love moist heat on their ass? Literally nobody, that's who.), and vats of ibuprofen and bourbon at the ready. My middle-aged body creaked and cracked, punished and protested. And my brandy-new soul told it to shut the fuck up. Because we were going back again tomorrow.

26 / on the death of my mother (or, so now what the fuck am i supposed to do?)

My mother is dead. *My mother is dead. My mother is dead.* Every day now, these words swirl around in my mind and in my mouth until they don't make sense anymore.

It's like when you stare at a word on a page for so long that it starts to look like nonsense and it makes you laugh because you know you know this word and yet, suddenly, it doesn't seem to stand for anything. And then you have to look away because you know you might lose the word forever if you don't. And when you look back at it with fresh eyes, it all makes sense again and it's just a word on a page. A word that you know.

But these words—*my mother is dead*—will never make sense now that they are true. They will never be words that I understand. I say them, over and over again, to remind myself. But that is not the same as understanding.

The last time I heard my mother's voice was in the parking lot of a Buffalo Wild Wings franchise, where I'd taken my friend's small son that night for his birthday. The small indignity of this is a stain on my heart and memory that will never come out, ever. My mom had called to say that she was having a "routine procedure" the next day. Outpatient. One that would make her feel better and have more energy to do the things she was enjoying again.

"If I get dead," she began ... this was something she said constantly—whether she was boarding a plane, going for a manicure, or taking a nap—and was usually followed by some inane instruction:

"Don't forget to refill your washer fluid."

"Don't forget about the smoked salmon in the refrigerator."

"Don't forget that anything below the waist is vulgar in polite conversation."

This was our routine—and holding up my end of the ridiculous bargain, I mocked her as I always did. "OK, Mom. If you get dead, I promise I'll remember that most people from Nevada are degenerates." And that was it. The last conversation I ever got to have with my mother. In a fucking parking lot.

She never woke up. There it is again, the nonsense noises in my brain: *She never woke up. My mother is dead. Anything below the waist is vulgar.* Again and again. Round and round. Nothing. It simply cannot be. These are not real words. Are they? Because if they are, it is the end of everything. If they are, I am rudderless, and I am alone. If they are, I am an orphan. I am an orphan.

I am an orphan.

I have always marveled at how, despite the magnitude of any personal tragedy, the world keeps spinning. Life around the loss just goes on as if it hadn't happened. As if your whole world had not simply ceased to exist in an instant. Days keep coming, nights keep falling, stores open, TV shows air, subways run, dogs crap on the floor, mail gets delivered.

Nothing, it seems, can kill the mundane infinity of things. Even my own body seems oblivious to my loss—it continues to wake up, to walk to the shower, to eat, to sleep, to cry, to *function*. How do they do this, the world and life and my body? Don't they fucking know that I am an orphan? Nothing should work anymore.

My mother is dead.

People don't know what to say. They try. But what they don't know is that loss like this changes you on a cellular level. That the world will forevermore be divided into categories of "people who understand" and "people who don't."

What they don't know is that no matter how much we get that it's said with love, if we ever hear the words "thoughts and prayers" again, we will fucking break something. And it will probably be your face. Say something different. Something that will help. Like "Wow, that sucks harder than a cow on a kitty teat." Or "Want to get drunk and cry?"

I am grateful, believe me, for the incredible outpouring of love from friends, no matter what form it takes. But I guarantee you that those on the "people who understand" list are not saying things like "thoughts and prayers." They are saying things like "I have marijuana. I will bring it to you."

Words were supposed to have been my gift, but now they fail me. Intake, output—my words don't work anymore. I can't find the ones I need and I can't shake the ones I don't want.

She never woke up.

I cannot describe the emptiness of my heart and the brokenness of my being in a way that makes sense to anyone else. I cannot describe the way that I wholly mistrust my decisions without my mother around to approve (erm, dictate) them. Or the secret fear that my brothers don't like me much at all and that, with our mom gone, they don't have to pretend anymore, ever. I can't properly report the way I feel physically crushed beneath the weight of the aloneness. I simply haven't the words.

I tell myself that I am brave. That I've done this before and I got through it. My father died and it was awful, but I survived. So why does it feel like I might not, this time?

I tell myself that I can live without her. I tell myself, as I reach for the phone without thinking, that I don't HAVE to call her anymore—that I can just think and she'll hear me. I tell other people that I am "hanging in there" or "taking it easy on myself" or some other bullshit that I expect they want to hear because it's easier for them than knowing the truth. But the truth is that the final, tiny piece of me that wasn't broken before is broken now. I am over. I am done.

She never woke up.

I am an orphan.

My mother is dead.

27 / haiti, babies, and the clap

I SHOULD HAVE perhaps called this "My Foray into International Adoption," but then I would have had to forego my (hopefully only) opportunity to include "the Clap" in a chapter title, which I was obviously not going to do. That would be like saying, "Oh, no thank you. I think I'll pass on the lifetime supply of original Twix bars." That would never happen either. Not on my watch.

So, yes. While I have never talked much about it publicly, there was a long while when this singular pursuit was my hell-bent (Jersey-style) full-time job. For about four months, I was tits-deep in The Process and nothing else. And by "process," I mean the rapey, ransacking inquest into my personal life, home, finances, emotions, and vagina. Yup. My vagina.

I had to provide *three separate agencies* with multiple ORIGINAL sets of tax returns (going back three years), bank statements, credit card bills, debts and assets, officially stamped valuations of my home/car/trust/IRA/real estate holdings, utility bills, passport/driver's license/social security card copies, multiple background checks (with fingerprinting), character witnesses (five), photographs (eight), certified divorce decrees (two), psychological evaluations (Yes, I passed. Asshole.), letters from my bank, letters from my accountant, letters from my local police, letters from my friends, letters from my family, letters of intent, letters to Haitian government officials, autobiographical statements, medical examinations (two), and home inspection reports. All notarized and copied many times over. All seen by several sets of strangers, including the pimply boob-staring guy at the copy shop.

In all my life, I had never felt so violated. Fuck, I had never BEEN so violated. I guess that makes me lucky.

Which brings us to the vagina part. Included in my two separate, notarized medical reports were the results of my laboratory tests for cholesterol, chlamydia, gonorrhea, syphilis, HIV, hepatitis A–C, and TB. (Yeah, um—1843 called. It wants its disease back. Did they want to test me for dropsy, too? How about plague? The vapors?)

Test me, bitches. Bring it right the fuck on. Because no matter what they threw at me next, I would hit that shit back at them hard enough to make their stupid, bureaucratic heads spin. They could probe my vadge like a goddamned unmanned *Titanic* rover and show every nosy notary and copy-shop guy on earth what they found in there.

Would that be enough? Would that give a starving orphan a chance for a loving home? Would THAT, finally, make me worthy of being someone's mother? If not that, then what?

It wasn't nearly over. I was only a few months into what could turn out to be a *three-year* process. And all that while, the babies in Haiti wasted away, cried for no one, died. They fucking died. While two different governments examined my finances, my psyche, my closets, and the contents of my vagina with a fine-toothed comb, the babies waited. They went unheld. And they died.

How is this OK? Especially when you consider the nonexistent screening process for biological birthers … oh, you're twelve? Super! What's that? You're a drug addict with three kids you can't take care of and you want to have another? Sure! How's that abusive relationship? Why not bring an emotionally doomed child into it?

For fuck's sake, you have to jump through more hoops to acquire a dog in this country than you do to have a natural child. No one asks any questions of birth mothers. No one looks at their bank statements. No one demands character witnesses. No one has to *deem them worthy*. Birth mothers don't have to notarize shit. Am I nuts (No! Yay! I just found out!), or is something very, very wrong here?

Wrong, inhumane, sadistic, invasive—whatever. It didn't matter. I would wait. I would jump when they said jump. I would give my blood and open my legs for the doctors and expose my home and net worth to strangers and I would have it all fucking notarized.

Because someday, someday, I would get to hold her and smell her skin and kiss her tears away and make her dinner and buy her onesies and sing her nonsense songs. Someday, the little girl named Babette who'd visited me in dreams ever since the 2010 earthquake would be my daughter, my joy, my hope, my *family*. She would be mine and I would be hers and we would be each other's. And I would wait because it was everything.

Because I had to believe that when I got the call, and got on the plane, and fell to my knees and took her up into my arms, maybe—just maybe—this would all be worth it. It had to be.

It had to be.

And then my mother died. Right in the middle of it.

My mother, who for once in her life was pleased and proud and happy for the decision I'd made and was ALL IN. My mother, who had bought my baby a dozen tiny dresses and three snowsuits and itty-bitty mittens because she knew she would be cold in the mountains until she got used to the climate. My mother, who learned some Creole so she could talk to my baby in words she might remember from her birth country. My mother, who'd been at bitter odds with me for most of my life, wanted this for me, and it made us closer. Little outfits. Tiny shoes. College funds. We could talk about these things with absolutely zero conflict, and it was amazing.

And she died.

I cannot fully explain the decision I made to withdraw my application. I can only say that, at the time, the grief was so monstrous and all-consuming that there was no room for a baby. I was so utterly unmoored at the prospect of running my own life that I had to start from scratch, and I knew I couldn't do it with a baby in my arms. So I gave her up. To save her.

Nowadays, I feign ambivalence about motherhood. I'm glad that I don't have to pay for anyone's college, I say. Or that I don't have to clean up human vomit. Or that being childless gives me unfettered time for awesomely idiotic pursuits (medieval sword fighting, anyone?). I say I'm glad that I didn't ruin anyone's life except my own.

Don't believe it for a minute. A mother was all I ever wanted to be.

My heart breaks all over again, still, every time I need something in the basement closet and see the wee dresses my mom sent hanging there, unworn. It takes my breath away.

My mother and my motherhood, both dead and gone; fashioned into frilly frocks and hidden away, out of sight.

28 / the severed heads aren't helping

Don't worry—this is not going to be some Cheryl Strayed–style account of hard-won redemption and triumph over the very grief that leveled me. It's just not—there's no redemption in sight, and certainly no triumph. I spent three months in some stranger's basement, for fuckssake—not to mention that said basement's every vertical surface was covered with the heads, skins, pelts, and antlers of things he'd personally killed for, I assume, fun.

Said basement had no internet or cable. Said basement had no kitchen. Aside from the whole "being indoors" thing, it was camping. I was lucky to have it, as I had nowhere else to go with my five pets—and I was grateful in a way that I kept needing to remind myself to be. Like, I was grateful not to be homeless. Which was not a small thing, but still. No fucking cable?

So, this might sound like psychiatric child's play, but: You should never up and move immediately after the sudden loss of a parent (thanks, Queen Obvious). Especially when you weren't planning to move and therefore have no fucking idea of where to go next or what to do when you get there. While selling my house to the guy who came out of nowhere and just *asked* if he could buy it seemed like a good idea at the time, I can tell you in hindsight that this was a seriously fucked-up thing to do.

I did it because that's what I do—I leave. That's how I handle pain, how I've *always* handled pain—I cut and run and never look back; and not in a theoretical or emotional way, which would allow me to stay conveniently stationed in my home whilst doing the cutting and running. Nope. I fucking relocate.

I sell houses that I just bought and move across the country to places I've never been and where I know no one. I start over, thinking the pain won't come with me or that it will somehow be less awful if the scenery around it is different. And this time it just dropped in my lap. It was the Universe clearly telling me, once again, to haul ass away from the sadness. Right?

The Things We Tell Ourselves.

Since 9/11/01, I have moved fifteen times. In twenty-three years. It does not take a genius to determine that this pervasive discontent with my surroundings is merely a reflection of the chaos that exists within me in my cells and the bloody, beefy lasagna of scar tissue over my heart from a life touched by far too much death. Illness, financial ruin, betrayal, relationship flame-outs: These things all hurt, too, and yes, I have fled from those as well, many times over.

But it's the death that really gets you.

If there's anything I should have learned from losing two parents, four grandparents, one uncle, one godmother, twenty-one close friends, and two boyfriends (All but the grandparents were sudden. The phone calls and news stories that I will never have the luxury of forgetting.), it's that there's no going around grief. You have to go through it. Much like the Fire Swamp in *The Princess Bride*: While it would be really, really nice to take the scenic belt loop around that shit and avoid the flame bursts, lightning sand, and ROUSs that you're pretty sure are going to kill you, make no mistake—that plan has its own set of perils. Better to risk the murdery marsh, with its well-documented dangers, and just get the fuck to the other side.

Which brings me back to the basement: the belly of the grief beast. My own personal Fire Swamp. Even though I got there, technically, by "running away again," I knew that this time, leaving was not going to be enough. So I went there intending to take the summer off from all the things I'd normally do to distract myself from the pain of losing my mother. What I didn't realize was that there were far many more of those things than I even realized, and that I couldn't do any of them even if I might have wanted to.

Aside from the obvious distractions like work, parties, committees, boys, booze, pills, clubs, and sports, I suddenly found myself with no kitchen, where I had always sought comfort—traveling, through food, to other worlds (i.e., far away from my own) without ever leaving the house.

No internet, where I might have spent vast, empty hours of time-suckage on Facebook or numbing out to teen vampire marathons on Netflix. No bathtub, where I'd surely be passing my evenings luxuriating with books and wine and the occasional inappropriate jet usage.

Friends there were few and far between. (In my experience, friends typically don't handle your grief well, anyway. They liked you the way you were, and you're not that way anymore. It's inconvenient for them, the fact that your entire world has caved in on top of you.) So I didn't see much of anyone at all.

I stopped playing roller derby. Although I still skated often, I skated alone. I ate alone. I walked alone. I went to the beach alone, if I went at all. I even stopped sexting with that adorable, too-young boy—not because it wasn't tons of fun, but because it was. I was going *through* it, goddammit, not around.

I was in self-imposed exile in some dude's basement with the looming specter of my dead mother and the heads of a dozen murdered animals to remind me why I was there and what I needed to do. Which was cry. Cry so hard that I choked on my own sobs and fought for breath through a gullet near-strangled by the sadness. Rage. Rest. Talk to people who were not there anymore. Forgive them. Forgive whichever god had a hand in this. Forgive myself.

Through it. Not around.

When summer ended, I would move to another lovely home in another lovely town where I would know no one. I would start over, as I always do. And while I liked to think that this time would be different because I'd forced myself to feel the pain fully, I didn't know that it would.

While I liked to imagine that the unbearable darkness of the Basement Days would ready me for a life better lived in the light, I didn't know that it would.

While I liked to dream that this experience would finally turn me into someone who believed that the things that didn't kill you made you stronger instead of someone who believed that those things chipped away at you little by little until there was almost nothing left, I didn't know that it would.

But I did know that when I left there, the worst would be behind me, and that I would have survived it, again. I would cook and skate and see friends and laugh and watch movies and mastur-bathe because those things should be for the living, not just for avoiding the dead.

I would try my hardest to stay in one place, no matter what happened, because I would know that running didn't fix it.

Through it, not around. And not away. Not anymore.

Wish me luck.

29 / thackery binx, emotional support chicken

A FEW YEARS ago, after moving to a wooded enclave outside Chicago and away from my last round of shitty neighbors (seriously, is it me?), I decided that I absolutely had to get some chickens—a curious decision on my part, as the only dealings I'd previously had with live poultry had left me bloodied, traumatized, and eating revenge nuggets with gleeful impunity.

First, my childhood pet Chico, who had spent his whole life following me around like a little chicken-shaped shadow and riding shotgun on my shoulder, decided one day he would please like to tear out my eyeball.

Straight outta nowhere one afternoon after school, he saw me, took a running start toward me, and, instead of jumping up onto my shoulder as per usual, did this insane, explosive, mid-air karate chicken-chop and caught the corner of my eye with his talon and dragged it down my face.

As you can imagine, my mother hen was displeased; I did not see Chico again and suspect I ate him for dinner that night. My scab was amazing and I remember pulling it off in one whole piece like one of those weird banana hairs and putting it, obviously, into my velvet skin box. With my other treasures. WHAT?

The second time, I was a twenty-three-year-old adult, and my brother had asked me to go check in on his animals while he and his wife were traveling. He'd moved to my grandpa's old sheep farm and kept all manner of creatures. He'd warned me that the rooster "might fuck with me" but I was honestly unconcerned. Animals loved me (people, not so much). I was their benevolent woodland queen and no species on earth would ever hurt me. I would come in doing some high-frequency chicken whispering and the rooster and I would be besties.

Spoiler alert: We were not besties. He tried to kill me.

He hid around corners and lurked, stalking me as I looked in on the sheep and pot-belly pigs. Once my guard was down, he took his shot: This motherfucker ran at me so hard and so fast, I literally did not see it coming until he was running up the side of my body like a squirrel up a tree, digging into my exposed summer skin for traction. There was a LOT of blood.

I always imagine this scene in an alternate-ending *Snow White*–like visual: *Me, smiling sweetly as I twirl, surrounded by tweeting birds and docile farm animals who simply bathe in my golden aura of pure goodness, knowing they are safe and loved. Then I get murdered by a chicken.*

The script needs some work.

So naturally, proving I am not one to dwell on the past, I now wanted my own tiny murder birds. I'd done some light chickensitting for one of my amazing new neighbors (who did not appear to hate me—yet—and who had assured me that there were no homicidal roosters involved), and realized to my astonishment that lady-chickens ... got me. Like chickens are so fucking weird that none of my bullshit even registered in their tiny chicken brains. I had to have them.

So one spring day, I came home with four baby chicks. Three one-day-old Buff Orpingtons that I named for the Sanderson sisters in *Hocus Pocus*, and a tiny black Silkie I called Binx, after the human ghost-cat that ultimately helps foil them. I was told by the store that they were 99 percent certain to be female, so that customers could be assured they'd never end up with an accidental male. Can you smell the foreshadowing?

Immediately, I was *obsessed*. They were sooo fucking cute. My stupid little fluff balls. I loved them irrationally. I truly, truly lost my shit over these fuckers. I spent all my time with them, just watching their weird little chicken world unfold and taking five hundred pictures a day to send to everyone I knew and pulling them around the neighborhood in a little wagon, just like you breeders do with your own hideous offspring.

All the chicks thrived except one—the little black Silkie. She was sickly, and about half the size of the others; every morning I held my breath when I went out to their heated box, not sure if she would have survived the night. I cuddled her, hand-fed her, cleaned her, held her, and talked to her for the whole summer, as she got stronger and fatter and started to hold her own with the others. She was my precious little buddy.

Around the same time—which likely explains why I instantly turned into a crazed chicken lady—I'd had a far-reaching fight with my remaining family that sent me into a very deep and unexpected depression. My default factory setting has always been melancholic, and I had had some mild depressive episodes in the past, but nothing like this. I had suffered from PTSD since the psycho-stalker-husband incident, so I think this time, the combination created a perfect storm of deadly sadness.

I was swallowed down into a darkness I'd never felt, as if

existing, undigested and alone, in the black belly of a giant whale that had forgotten to chew its food. The pain was so deep and so constant that I began to contemplate ending it for good; for my own benefit and for the family I'd hurt with my recklessness. It seemed that I'd never feel light or happy or unburdened again, and I longed to be free of it. Forever. Anthony Bourdain had just done it. So had Kate Spade. I envied them.

As my thoughts inched ever-closer to that dark edge, I inevitably thought of Binx, the little black hen who had become my charge, my focus, and my Reason. She needed me, and while I could think of plenty of other people who could care for my dogs and cats if I took my leave, I could not think of anyone who would continue to love and care for Binxie the way she needed to be cared for. So I never made it to that edge. Her vulnerability made me see past the selfishness of a "permanent solution" and focus on getting through it. That little black Koosh ball was the only thing standing between me and the abyss, and it was enough.

The tiny black hen had saved my life, quite literally. She gave me purpose when she was unwell, and profound comfort when I was. So by the time "she" began cock-a-doodle-doo-ing later that fall, I could not—would not—imagine my life without her/him. (My asshole friends made relentless jokes about me ending up with a trans chicken, because of course I did. Very on-brand.) I think, if possible, I loved him even more for being a boy chicken—for being something other than he was supposed to be, through no fault of his own. I felt that shit in my soul, and vowed to protect him fiercely. Now he napped in my lap, nuzzled my ear with tiny nibbles, sang the Song of His People in his tiny adolescent boy-voice, and followed me around the yard just like a faithful dog. He was my whole heart, which itself was healing every day thanks to Binx's wee majesty. The darkness inside me faded to a mere shadow and I felt hopeful. Lighter. I was going to be OK.

Everybody loved Binx, and my wonderful neighbors assured me that he did not bother them at all (I also plied them with fresh eggs from Binx's hardworking sister witches, which I'm sure helped). He slept inside at night so that his morning crows would not disturb anyone.

Inevitably, though, I got the phone call from the police that I'd dreaded from the moment his first little choked cock-a-doodle came out: Some motherfucking City Council Karen had complained about the crowing, and I would have to get rid of my rooster.

I THINK THE FUCK NOT.

My every primal, motherly, protective, and Jersey-fed Five-Families instinct kicked in and I was on fire with dread and vengeance. I was NOT getting rid of him. I didn't give a rat's red ass about "laws" and "noise ordinances." Fuck with my chicken at your own peril, motherfuckers.

Fuck around with *me* and find out.

Despite my posturing and the melodramatic revenge porn running in my head, I was scared. I was so, so scared. I couldn't lose him. My Binxie. I'd literally move before I let that happen. I enlisted a realtor to show me some farms in Wisconsin, where no one would bat an eyelash at my rooster's beautiful music. Turned out, rural Wisconsin is a blood-red hotbed of farm owners whose undying love for Donald Trump was proclaimed by painting his name on every barn in sight. I'd eat a bag of hair before I'd inhabit that hellscape. And I was certainly not going to raise my chicken in a place whose core values were so divergent from my own. He'd never get a play date, and we'd be excluded from every hoedown and Klan rally in town. (Relax, Wisconsin. I'm just being a dick. I know you don't actually attend hoedowns.) I needed to think of something else.

Which I did. Not too long after the farm-shopping debacle, I sat bolt-upright in the middle of the night with a dramatic gasp, practically lifted off the bed by the magnitude of my own brilliance. The ever-present dread left my body in a rush of relief and euphoria, as I knew, finally, how I would save my chicken and stick it to the Man. In the nighttime silence, I got out of bed and crept to my office with all of the diabolical, hand-rubbing treachery my dark heart could conjure. There, I googled "how to register an emotional support animal" and I knew I had won.

Hail the Old Gods. I am an evil genius. I registered him right then and there (the best thing my horrible ex-husband ever gave me was that PTSD, now sitting in my medical records as proof that I needed emotional support), and just like that, they could not touch me. A few days later, Binx's certificate arrived in the mail, along with his name tag and photo ID card, announcing him as an official Emotional Support Chicken. I could take him on a plane, or to a restaurant, or rent a no-animals-policy apartment for me and my chicken if I wanted to —which would be *amazing*, I grant you—but right then I simply didn't want to lose him. He was safe. Also? Sickest burn ever, amirite?

Fuck you, local-government Karen! Guess what? I am fucking crazy! Utterly unhinged! This official paper I bought from the internet says so. I could literally lose my shit at any time. I know who you are and where you live. You wanna see what happens when you take the crazy lady's pet chicken away? Didn't think so.

Whore.

Binx only lived another year after all that. Two in total. One summer evening, as I always did, I put him to bed and told him he was my most special boy and that I loved him forever. I kissed him on his little walnut, thanked him for being my best buddy, and promised I'd always take care of him. The same speech I repeated every night as I brought him inside for his bedtime. When I checked on him before I went to sleep, he was gone. It had only been an hour or so since I'd left him. He must have already been dying when I brought him inside. I'm so glad I got to have one last bedtime with him.

Binx had always been sort of sickly, and honestly would have likely died in his first week if I had not been so singularly focused on saving him. I can see this now (four years later) and keep the emotional meltdown to thermonuclear-adjacent when I think of him. But at the time, the grief was cataclysmic. I swore off loving anything ever again. I would never get another pet and I would never change my mind. I knew I'd go through similar pain as my ten remaining animals eventually and inevitably joined Binx in the crowded pet cemetery of my soul, but on that night, I promised myself I would never willingly sign up for this again. Too many haymakers to the heart. For the first time in my whole life, I vowed to be pet-free someday. I'm sticking by it.

I wondered if, now that Binx was gone, I would return to the darkness where I'd lived that previous summer, certain that the world would be better without me. He didn't need me here anymore, and I feared that my broken brain might convince me once again that no one did. But it didn't happen. Beyond the crippling grief and shock, I was OK. Binx had healed my heart before he'd broken it again; I was stronger and better because of him, and I would survive this.

Maybe he only stuck around as long as he had to to make sure I'd be OK. Maybe I needed to love something so fiercely and irrationally that I could finally find some compassion in my heart for what my own mother suffered. Because I did. She loved me so much that the thought of losing me pushed her into a madness that swallowed her whole. I get it now, and my heart hurts for her. Her life must have been hell.

In true, next-level-crazy fashion, I had Binx taxidermied. I wanted him with me always, to remind me to be strong and to remember the love we shared. It took months to stuff that tiny chicken. When I finally brought him home, I had a good cry and placed him high up on a shelf in my office, out of reach of the basically feral pack of dogs that own my house. He didn't last a week. Those assholes performed some coordinated Cirque du Soleil shit and destroyed my stuffed Binxie in two minutes flat.

It made me feel pretty good about my decision to stop having pets.

And in case you are wondering, no. I will not be taxidermying my dogs.

30 / wheels (how roller derby saved my soul)

When I put on my first pair of roller skates in 2012, I had recently been divorced from, stalked by, and catfished by an emotional terrorist who simply would not stop. Bullying, berating, begging. You know the story. Battered to exhaustion by his madness, I had long teetered dangerously on the edge of surrender, but I had, in the end, survived a full-on, years-long assault by a master manipulator. But barely.

I needed saving. And I'd chosen roller derby to do the honors. Let's fucking go.

The thing is, *roller skating is really fucking hard*. Damn my mother and her masher fixation for withholding this simple pleasure in my childhood, when learning was easy. I was in no way prepared for how bad I would be at this.

My first night on skates was an orgy of pain and humiliation that I'd never felt in my entire well-behaved, self-controlled life. *I cried in front of strangers.* The searing agony of fall after fall onto cold concrete was incidental. The searing agony of abject embarrassment was far worse. The women running the practice—my future soul sisters—would later tell me they were absolutely certain I'd hobble away from the track that night, never to return.

But I did return. I went back despite the pain and shame, and despite my heartbreaking lack of talent on roller skates. You must understand: I don't *do* things that I don't do very, very well. My vanity, my ego, the insistence on my own perfection do not typically indulge me with chances to make an ass of myself, especially more than once. I credit the catastrophic structural damage my psyche had sustained for letting me slip through those ass-making cracks just this once.

I made an ass of myself like a fucking BOSS. But, dear friend, I also saved my soul.

Because, as it happens, by the time I put my first pair of skates on, I had also been at war with my body—not just my mother—for most of my life. I had loathed it, cursed it, dishonored and abused it. I had starved it, gorged it, purged it, damned and shamed it for decades. It was not thin. It was not lithe and lovely, like other girls'. It was too big. Too tall, too muscular. *It was FAT.* It was my life's secret shame—my too-big body and the awful things I did to it to try to make it beautiful.

But you don't have to be thin or beautiful to play roller derby. And one day, shortly after that first time, I realized I was falling less. When I did fall, it was easier to get up. There was less crying. I was not so sore anymore. My body was getting stronger, more resilient. Shit, *I* was getting stronger and more resilient. I was less afraid, not just of skating but of *everything*.

Out of nowhere, I suddenly cared infinitely more about being powerful than I did about being thin. And I was proud of myself. Holy fuck. *I was proud of myself.*

I began to silently thank my legs for pushing me around the track lap after lap, my heart for working harder than ever before, and my lungs for giving me the air I needed to fly. As my thighs grew thicker under my jeans, I found myself not recoiling at their size, but rejoicing in their strength.

I began to eat when I was hungry and stop when I was full. My step grew surer even in shoes that didn't have wheels on them. I gave fewer fucks. I was part of something special and I began to grasp that I, too, was something special, despite my measurements.

This extraordinary new understanding—this new LIFE—was a gift from the very thing I had attempted to beat into bony submission for most of its days. The irony is not lost on me—just as I myself had narrowly escaped the clutches of an evil overlord who tried and failed to crush me, so had my body.

I am ever grateful to us both for not surrendering.

In derby, the reason you come is not always the reason you stay. You almost always find things you didn't know you were looking for. Derby gave me strength and grit and courage. It gave me back the power that I had myself given away. It gave me sisterhood and drive and a million things that I am grateful for every single day. But roller derby did not really save my soul, in the end. It made me able, fearlessly and finally, to save my own.

Now, in my mid-fifties, my derby career is over. I've had fourteen orthopedic surgeries, including a total knee replacement. Every single one of them was worth it. My derby relationships are among the strongest and realest that I have, and there's a reason for that: Those friendships were all built on absolute authenticity, because you don't have to hide anything in derby. My sisters and brothers in the game all found their ways there the same way I did: by not really fitting in anywhere else. By being too strange for other sports and other circles. By finding the place that would have us.

Nowadays, I am a coach for the next generation of derby

players. My skaters range in age from seven to seventeen; after that, they're eligible for the adult league. I wish I could express the supreme joy I find in welcoming these wee ones into the derby community. Into a world where they can be anything they want. Where they can craft an identity that perfectly captures their essence without apology or censure. Where they learn to skate, certainly, but where they also learn to decide who they're going to be.

It's a world where being fierce is fundamental. Where differences are celebrated, not suppressed. Where girls are given agency over their bodies and their minds. Where they are given permission to not take any shit. Now or ever.

Where danger is part of the deal, and dealt with accordingly.

This is why I do it.

I do it because when I was that age, I didn't have anyone to give me those gifts. I was not encouraged, embraced, or accepted for the magical weirdo I was and the even more magical weirdo I would become. I was boxed and stunted, regulated and controlled. Like veal.

And you'd best believe that if I'd had that single voice in my ear telling me I could do anything, be anything, build anything, and dream anything, my life would have turned out very differently.

I do it because I get to be that voice for them, in case they need to hear it, too. So maybe—just maybe—their souls won't need saving, because they learned early to believe in their power.

There will be no veal on my watch.

31 / feathers from charlie

I SPENT AN ill-fated and terribly lonely year at boarding school when I was a freshman in high school. (This is bullshit; can we please normalize freshperson now, patriarchy?) My parents had become concerned that I was spending too much time with the Fast Crowd (they literally called it that) and was careening down the acne-pocked express lane to teen ribaldry. Boys were starting to call around. Some of them *not even WASPs.*

I was a handful, not because I was bad or disobedient, but because I wanted to be, desperately, or so I thought. It was starting to occur to me that not all homes were like mine: the rules, the repression, the rage; other kids were starting to go to parties *with no parents* (fetch my pearls, Basil, I must clutch them!). I was locked in my room, practice-kissing on my Adam Ant poster, when my parents weren't looking (and when I finally wore out the mouth-hole on Fonzie), and when they were, I was sullenly advertising my inner mutiny with my face.

So they sent me away. I should have been elated.

Girls' boarding school in Connecticut is exactly what you imagine it is. Probably worse, especially in the early eighties. Rich kids who lived in their privilege and fended for themselves, most of them years into their away-from-home schooling by age fourteen. They were already drinking, smoking ciggies and weed, and Doing the Sex. I was not.

My folks thought they were sending me someplace where my parentally-mandated virtues would be groomed and celebrated (or, at the very least, remain intact); where they *actually* sent me was to a bacchanal teen orgy of drugs, rebellion, and mean-girl politics run by husky-voiced field hockey players who were merciless in their derision of all things unworldly or wholesome. I was both, and therefore, I was lunch.

While of course now I wonder why I didn't *fucking love it there*, then, I was miserable. I had only a couple of friends, some upperclassmen (Jesus Christ, even at a fucking girls' school?!) who took pity on me and one girl my age—I'll call her Avril—whose effortless, Jackie-O coolness could withstand her association with me, the girl with the Boy George decor. I could never figure out why she wanted to be my friend, but despite receiving handwritten notes from several mean girls outlining all the reasons she should not be and how her social currency would surely plummet if she continued to consort with me (Really. I saw them.), she did. *Looking at you, Veronica Robertson.*

One early-spring Sunday, Avril and I went "downtown," which was actually just a strip mall halfway between our school and our male counterpart in the next town. We were hoping to see some boys. Correction: *I* was hoping to see some boys. Avril was already dating college-age men and had very little time for the pimply teens whose wet-mouthed fumblings meant dry-humping behind the mall for ten seconds until they jizzed in their pleated chinos.

But there was one boy who even Avril agreed was worth the hormonal hype surrounding him at every co-ed affair between our two schools. Charlie. So far out of my particular league I had only ever seen him from afar, while I lurked alone in a dark corner at a school dance, sucking my braces and wondering what it must be like to talk to someone like that without barfing.

On this very spring Sunday, immediately after I had tripped, fallen down, and taken an entire beach ball display down with me, Charlie (!!!) walked into the CVS where I was sprawled on the dirty gray carpet in a raucous heap of beach-ballery. Avril knew Charlie, of course, from Being Cool, and greeted him and his friends accordingly. I, on the other hand, flailed wildly on the ground in an attempt to extract myself from the beach ball situation and find someplace to immediately go kill myself. The boys were polite—bemused, even?—through introductions, and after engaging in some small talk with Avril while I crouched there, frozen in horror, they went on their way.

And then everything changed.

The next morning, an extremely cool older girl approached me in the dining hall. Naturally, I was terrified. She must have read the code-red fear on my face or, more likely, with her advanced mean-girl prey drive, she could smell it.

"Relax," she said. "I just want to talk."

I did not relax.

"O-oh-OK. W-what's up?" I choked.

"Charlie likes you. He asked my boyfriend to find out who you were and see if you would want to meet up sometime. I'm just delivering the message."

I immediately started tearing up, certain this was a trick or a trap; a sadistic setup that would begin with me thinking I was meeting the boy of my dreams and end with me naked and covered in pig's blood in the woods while the becloaked mean girls' chorus cackled diabolically. "What did I ever do to you?" I snarfled.

"Um, nothing? So can Charlie call you or what?"

I nodded, sheepish and unconvinced.

That was Monday.

By Friday, I was popular. Off-limits to my tormentors. Word had gotten out. Charlie had called me twice that week, and I'd be seeing him that weekend. Charlie, the golden teen God of Preparatory Education. Charlie, the flowy-haired lacrosse star. Charlie, the epicenter of everywhere I'd ever wanted to be. THE Charlie.

My Charlie.

Charlie and I embarked that spring on what would be a thirty-six-year relationship. We dated, broke up, reconciled, broke up, met up for magical interludes, and disappeared from each other's lives intermittently while we dabbled in other loves and other lives. Sent each other to hell and back straight through college. Eventually, we settled into a forever friendship; profound on its own but always, always simmering with the whiff of possibility. Nay, the *certainty* of possibility.

Certainty that when all the bullshit was done, we thought ... after all of it—marriages, kids, middle age, mortgages, divorces, psycho exes—we'd find our way back and it would be us at the end. Like lobsters.

Charlie died, almost four years ago. I found out from Google, after he missed my birthday. He never missed my birthday.

I am ill-prepared to describe the depth of my grief and don't suppose I'll even try. The pain can bring me to my knees, still. In a life that's been heavy with loss, this is The One. The fucking *weight* of it, my god. My greatest love; my maybe-happy ending. Gone. Texts unread, calls unanswered. He's just gone.

A month or so after I found out, I took my bedtime pot gummy and tucked in, waiting for the heavy hug of the THC to descend, wrapping me in the weighted blanket of a mostly dreamless sleep. But it didn't come. So I started talking to Charlie. As one does. Mind you, I am nuts, but I am not *that* kind of nuts. I don't make a habit of talking out loud to dead people (or any people, for that matter), but it just happened.

I talked to him long into the night, offering amends for some flimsy teen slights, recalling oddball adventures, reminding him of the beautiful days.

"Remember that one Dead show," I asked the silence, "the one where we held hands and laughed and twirled for hours? So in love that when Tisha was tripping balls, she kept asking nearby people if they could see the blue laser beams connecting our souls?" Laughing, crying, calling out into the dark bedroom.

"WHERE ARE YOU?!" I finally screamed. "Why can't I feel you? Just tell me when you're here. Tell me how I'll know."

Exhausting myself at last, I began to drift into the in-between, where dreams threaten but you still can stop them with a quick return to consciousness if you don't like where they're headed. There he was, my Charlie. Aged about twenty, sitting in a glowing golden field, resplendent. His smile lit with the purest joy; love undulated all around him like summer heat pulsing on blacktop.

I didn't want to wake up. Except I was awake. *What the fuck is happening, what the fuck, what the fucking FUCK?* Then his grin grew bigger and he waved his hands as if above some imaginary cauldron, but instead of gherkin-and-goatball vengeance stew bubbling beneath them (that's what's usually bubbling in my cauldron, anyway), there were feathers. Lilting, swirling, silently dancing feathers. For me.

"Thank you," I whispered.

Wow, I thought the next morning. *That was one hell of a gummy*. Probably? But part of me knew it was more than that.

My brothers had both previously reported similar (like VERY similar) moments with our dead mother. I didn't believe them—she had never appeared to me and since I was OBVIOUSLY HER FAVORITE I knew she would have if she were making the ghost rounds. Besides, I'm smart. I'm a Science Person. Show me proof or fuck right off. It was a lovely little trip, but I decided grief is its own ghost and does fucked-up things to people on drugs.

But two days later, there it was. A perfect, pristine blue jay feather, expertly placed in my path out to the chicken coop, which I walk several times a day because I am a lunatic in literal love with her chickens (it was understood in the vision, somehow, that chicken feathers would not be part of the visitation proceedings). I surprise-party screamed, picked up my precious blue feather, and felt more joy, more life, more certainty, and more hope than I maybe ever had. I laughed and cried and jumped around on the lawn like the aforementioned lunatic I am. My neighbors are used to it by now.

Charlie sent me a feather. My Charlie.

Since then, I have found hundreds. Several a day, sometimes. It doesn't matter where I am. I've even found them *inside my house* when I know they had not been there moments before. There was one inside a sealed parcel containing my quarterly bean club cache. (Yes, I am in a bean club. Don't be jealous.) They are mostly blue jay feathers but not always. If I had kept them all, I could easily have made a fabulous boa or some feather pants out of them. But then I'd have to go to Coachella. Never mind.

Look, I don't know if I believe any of it. And I certainly don't give a fuck if anyone else believes it. I constantly play skeptical games of "that one doesn't count" or "yeah, but that's roadkill." Of course I do. Am I seeing them because I'm looking for them? Probably.

But I don't recall ever finding a feather before, ever, despite working at a raptor center for years. The one thing I do know for certain is that when I find my feathers, I am less singularly lost to my grief. I am comforted, and am allowed, for just a moment, to toy with the notion of everlasting love. Of connection that transcends every bit of bullshit we throw to try to break it. Bonds that survive the severing of them. Life after death or life in death, or even just *my* life after *his* death. I'm still here and I need him to be, too.

So I will believe. And not believe. But mostly believe, because it's the gentler choice. Because Charlie would want me to show myself that small kindness. Because unless or until we meet again, it's all I have of him. Because I must.

Never stop sending me feathers, Charlie.

My Charlie.

32 / dear big brothers

I AM NOT sure I've ever properly thanked you. For being my brothers and my friends—the best of friends now, actually. For being generally awesome and pretty damn cool for a couple of old farts. You know it'd be awkward as shit if I tried to do it with my mouth hole, so I'm doing it here, where there's a delete button for when I screw it up. Here goes:

Thank you. You fuckers are the absolute best.

I am a huge pain in the ass. I know I test your patience on the regular, and I'm sorry for that. I'm still figuring out how to be a legit grown-up. Thank you for your understanding, as I am still learning to navigate the world without Mom; it's not been as easy for me as I hoped it would.

I also know that me coming along when I did—twelve and ten years, respectively, after you guys—was annoying and ridiculous. I mean, who needed a goddamn baby in the house when your lives were already well underway? (I was pretty fucking cute, though, you gotta admit.)

You guys were kind to me—mostly—when all I did was buzz around you like an extremely adorable mosquito. I was a little squirt who just wanted to be near you, my very own 1970s shaggy-haired superheroes. I remember every single time you took me for ice cream or to the movies, because I knew I was the luckiest little fuck on earth. But with the age difference, there was no way for us to really know each other back then. So I'm extra grateful that we know each other now.

Billy, you welcome all of us into your heart and home without a second thought, and will go to all ends in order to help someone who needs it. You're so like Mom in that way. The best way. Your home—once Grampa's beloved sheep farm—is the soul of our family. You guard our last remaining legacy with your very life, protecting it and preserving it for the love of our ancestors and as an homage to the happiest of family times; in your care, those happy times are still as vibrant and alive as they were back then. You do it for all of us: cousins, in-laws, friends, friends of friends, random kids, the guy who works at the post office ...

You are an incredible friend and husband, and I swear to God, the last man on earth who stands up from his seat at the dinner table when one of us ladyfolk returns from whatever nose-powdering or bowl-murdering went on in the restroom.

You took me to my very first concert—Bruuuuuce—when you surely had other and better options (like literally *anyone* else). It was probably the last thing you wanted to do—take an idiot fourteen-year-old to see the freaking BOSS—but you did. Who does that??! Amazing big brothers, that's who.

And Archie, you have given me the greatest gift of my life in your three magnificent daughters. You, sir, made me an auntie, which is the very best thing that I am. And the reason they're as absurdly smashing as they are is due, in no small part, to the kind of dad you've been. You encourage them, protect them, and let them figure out who they are on their own. And they are spectacular. Literally my favorite humans on this earth.

I have always marveled at your closeness with them because we three didn't grow up that way. It must have taken you wayyyy out of your comfort zone to be so open with them and allow them to be open with you. But you did it. You knew it was important to break the cycle of don't ask/don't tell parenting, and you did.

Plus? You've always been the coolest cat around. Smart, athletic, and effortlessly funny. Damn, dude. You fucking rock.

I am obviously the ridiculous one. The Drama Queen and certified loose cannon. It's embarrassing, I know. But this here loose cannon will protect us, our family, with every ounce of unhinged loyalty I carry in my soul. You have my word as a crazy person, I will CUT a bitch, with glee, to defend your brotherly honor.

I will hide the bodies and burn the evidence if ever you need help out of that particular pickle, which I don't necessarily foresee. But you never know. If it's some blistering, well-aimed word-murder you need, I got you. Need me to throw hands? You know I will. Medieval Viking weaponry? I've got that, too, and I know how to use it (I think ... you just, like ... swing it, right?) Ain't nobody messing with my big brothers.

So thanks, for being the best brothers ever. It can't have been easy.

I love you, assholes.

33 / the mess of me

Well shit, my friend. We made it. You've stuck by my crazy ass for the duration of this literary wilding for what feels, I'm certain, like approximately three hundred years. I'm grateful that you've stayed with me through the ridiculous *Sturm und Drang,* the ups and downs, the twists and the turds. Friends for life, I tell you. Thanks for tolerating my epic amount of bullshit and letting me tell you my story. If it has made you feel even slightly better about your own, then fuckin' A. That's a beautiful thing.

It's been eleven years now since my mother died. They have been hard ones, certainly, but also weirdly triumphant, in a Lifetime movie kind of way (assuming Lifetime is now peddling poop porn and vagina toes). I mean, I'm free, for fuckssake! That is no small thing for a dickhead like me.

I have done allll the things that would have horrified my poor mother, and I've done them with relish. Roller skating, sexting, piercing questionable body parts, outsmarting municipal government twats (actually, she would have loved that one) ... My orphanhood has not disappointed.

But it's still confusing as hell sometimes. The grief of losing her and the damage she wrought while she was here are unfaltering in their bitter, ever-present rivalry. I have come to understand, though—with significant relief—that I can be both sad that she is gone *and* resentful as fuck at the mess she made of me. Both can be true. I don't have to choose.

Eleven years on, and I am healing—from her death, sure, but more importantly, from her goddamn *life*. My mother's was a soul so tormented that it would not, could not help itself; so on fire with rage and fear that devastation was the only possible outcome. Scorched earth for everyone (in my brain right now, I am Oprah, gleefully yelling, "*You get scorched earth! You get scorched earth! And YOU get scorched earth!*"). That shit was no joke, and rising up from the ruin has been an all-hands-on-deck military operation.

I hope I've convinced you that my mother had real, raw love in her heart and bottomless empathy for any creature that was in pain; that she did everything in her power to lessen others' suffering, from animals to perfect strangers. It's true. Which made it all the more difficult to abide the prodigious amount of suffering that she herself created. This has been the unwinnable tug of war of my life; the inexorable, warring truths of who my mother was. How the fuck do I make sense of that?

Therapy. Accountability. Roller derby. Emotional support poultry.

That's how.

I am learning to reconcile the kind, generous, loving person she was at her core with the forces that kept those things trapped under the rubble of her mind's own earthquakes. I am learning, slowly, to separate her essence from her illness.

These have been years of figuring out who and what I am, without her simply deciding for me. I never really had a say in the matter before, and it's still blowing my mind a little that I get to decide that shit for myself. That I don't have to hide things from people I love or fear the wrath of their disfavor. That I can fart and cry and blow my nose in my shirt and know that my chosen family of fuckheads will love me anyway. That I can go about cleaning up the mess of me in whatever way I choose—and that no one can or will do it for me.

Years of learning to love the parts of myself that she could not, and forgiving myself for being *weird* or *difficult* or *awkward* —how, pray tell, could I have been anything else? I didn't stand a goddamn chance. Years spent allowing myself to be the ridiculous wreck that I am, in all my filthy, foul-mouthed glory. Radical self-acceptance—I highly recommend it.

It's been eleven years of simply learning how to support my grown-ass self. Figuring out how to live without the weekly wads of cash that arrived in the mail and the absurd spread of platinum cards in my wallet that she urged me to use with impunity. (Mom was always trying to outsmart the government and their pesky financial regulations—her money was for her children, she said, not for the *GODDAMNED IRS*. My penchant for Sticking It to the Man, as it turns out, is my birthright.) Swallowing my pride and selling her jewelry for cash, because I did not know what else to do. It's been a real kick in the ladyballs, if I'm being honest.

Years spent figuring out what I might like to be and what I might be good at, and that maybe those answers were one and the same (and no, it's not "being an asshole," you jerk). Going back to school and starting, at age fifty, the career I abandoned thirty years ago, before it even started. Getting my ass its very own marketable skill, thank you very much.

blows on finger guns victoriously

It's more than a little bit heartbreaking how proud I am of myself for unlocking this most basic, level-one adult achievement. I am very aware that it is pathetic and nauseating: *Poor little spoiled brat has to go get a job, better call the waaahhhmbu-*

lance. I promise you, I know. And the shame I carry for acquiescing to our sick "Behave yourself and I'll make it worth your while" contract will never fully fade. I will cringe at that for all eternity. But I'm still proud of the work I've done to start over. It's never too late to decide to be a fucking grown-up, I guess, although I suspect that shit's highly overrated.

Years, too, of some pretty dreadful regret. For the times I was unkind and for failing to find compassion for my mother and the catastrophic glitch in her wiring that, when combined with her own trauma, unleashed a godless nether-hell upon all those around her. For the four decades I lost wishing I had a different mother instead of trying to figure out how to love the one I had. For keeping things from her that would have given her an opportunity to really know me (not the sexting, though, you perv), because it didn't seem worth the risk. For hiding my joys and pains and not giving her the chance to surprise me by maybe understanding. OK, no. You're right, terrible idea.

For not trusting her to love me even if I wasn't who she wished I'd be.

It's been eleven fucking years of learning to forgive her for the things she could not help and, even more crushingly, for the things she would not help. For eschewing the medicine that had given us brief glimpses (before she realized what she was taking) of the sweet soul we knew was in there, underneath the hell demons. For not sacrificing her pride and embracing treatment for the sake of the children she claimed to love so much. For hurting us. For embarrassing us. For breaking us. For leaving us.

It's a lot to forgive. Booze helps.

After eleven years, I've come to settle in a place of hard-won, grumpy-ass gratitude for the grief that is my strange, unsought superpower—how it has softened my sharp edges and quieted my soul's own anarchy. I am grateful for the life and lessons my mother gave me, even the shitty ones.

I'm even grateful for the kinda gross privilege of my past, which I simultaneously resent and still secretly long for. Just to be safe, I've since covered my body in beautiful, sprawling tattoos, ensuring that no country club or debutante ball would ever have me again. Terrifying the pearl-clutchers is just good, clean fun if you ask me.

I unequivocally owe my life to therapy, and my sanity to the hell-bent fury with which I've pursued it. Seriously. My crazy didn't stand a fucking chance. I am intensely grateful for my remaining family, and the many magnificent miscreants who have held my hand and walked with me through this long reckoning, through this soft settling of my heart's accounts.

I am grateful for my own juxtapositions and contradictions; I am equal parts choice and circumstance—roller derby and Robert Frost, turd talk and tea sandwiches—and leaning more heavily toward "choice" all the time.

I'm getting there.

acknowledgments

OK, REAL TALK, mofos. This book would not exist without the fierce and tireless support of the many gorgeously gifted grown-ups in charge of keeping my ass in line: primarily, my Rising Authors homies Ami Hendrickson, Rose Friel, Hussein al-Baiaty, Christian Dufner, and Chas Hoppe—it's been a true fucking thrill rolling dirty with you all; my Life to Paper publishing parents Tabitha Rose and Donald Loney ... thanks for believing this memoir mattered, and for letting me have my Oxford commas (sorry about all the cursing); Becca Kadison and Sue (Tsunami) Sumeraj; the brilliant author Kerry Kletter, who literally made me do it; all the generous (and possibly deranged) souls who offered help, encouragement, connections, and enthusiasm for this weird little book—John Garbarino, Jason Campbell, Sharona Wilhelm, Shane DuBow, Claudia (Cookie) Kozma-Kaplan, Kris Koval, Andy Frye, David Rynne, Peggy Pillmore, Ken Mason, Alec Schwartz, and Col. Lee T. Guzofski.

The various ride-or-die ruffians and reprobates that make my life worth living: Kim Gore, Carl "Scoreson Welles" Cutler, Victoria Saunders, Dawn Grace, Vince Bozman, the Owen family, Alan Zablocki, Laura Cunningham, Madeleine

Mazanek, Paula Burzawa, Tiffany McKenna, Ashley Borg, Mel Pfister, Heather "Barb Dwyer" Fitch, my sweet cuzzies Helen Bonzulak and Dana Koenig, Kristen Stavola, Rich Lalley and all my Rotary brethren, GFN/HOF/SOH, Jen Stephens and Dave Block, Abby Smith, Sarah Berry, Marc Speziale, Joy and Mike Monahan, Sara Pfitzinger, and Aasim Chowdhry.

My therapist, Dr. Suzanne Drake: for your endless patience, masterful handling, cutting-edge bullshit barometer, and intuitive healing mojo. You're a goddamn saint.

To my bros, Bill "Beelzebub" and John "Archie" Kuipers, their (wayyyyy) better halves Dawn and Cyd Kuipers, and Bill Horton, our brother from another mother: thanks for (mostly) tolerating me. No small feat, that.

Ted and Nick Peterson: for sharing your grief with me and letting me share mine with you—thank you. You fuckers are family now.

And to Charlie, my Charlie. For the feathers.

about the author

Marie Kuipers is the "Grammar Hammer," an eagle-eyed copy editor and proofreader dedicated to fine-tuning even the clunkiest prose, making it purr like a horny cougar. She graduated from Georgetown University two hundred years ago and holds an editing certification from the prestigious University of Chicago Graham School, which, according to her mother, makes her "unemployable." She lives with an assortment of flatulent dogs and coddled chickens near Chicago, where she coaches junior roller derby while still longing for New Jersey and its dubious assortment of encased meats. This is her first book.

Made in the USA
Monee, IL
20 October 2024

68359748R00108